Edward D Holton

Travels with Jottings

From Midland to the Pacific

Edward D Holton

Travels with Jottings

From Midland to the Pacific

ISBN/EAN: 9783743313804

Manufactured in Europe, USA, Canada, Australia, Japa

Cover: Foto ©Andreas Hilbeck / pixelio.de

Manufactured and distributed by brebook publishing software (www.brebook.com)

Edward D Holton

Travels with Jottings

LETTER I.

Canon City—Journey Across Iowa and Kansas.

CANON CITY, Colorado, December 16, 1879.

Three weeks to-morrow marks the time since, with my wife and little grandson (a lad six years old), I left our good city on a tramp to the Pacific Coast with no other object—save some considerations of health for the little boy—than to mark with one's own eyes, the marvelous strides which our republican civilization has made between the shores of Lake Michigan and the coast of the Pacific Ocean and the fortieth and forty-fifth degree of north latitude, within that period of time when in my young manhood I became a citizen of the then little village of Milwaukee now so grand, so strong, and beautiful a city. Our first stop was made at Delavan, where we took our thanksgiving dinner with the large family of one hundred and fifty mute children—and a happier family you will seldom find. In passing, I am happy to say that the improvised buildings made by the trustees of this Institution since the great calamity of the fire, were so far in use as to promise safety and comfort to the large number of inmates, and afford almost undiminished facilities for the prosecution of the great purposes for which the institution was founded, to-wit: the education of this unfortunate but deeply interesting class of children of the State, who cannot be educated in the public schools.

On our first night from home we enjoy the hospitalities of a friend at the royal little city of Beloit in our own State, where industry, peace, plenty, virtue and knowledge are enthroned in her valleys and upon her hilltops. Our next stop is at the thriving city of Dubuque, with which we ought long since to have been in direct railroad connection by the extension of the Monroe Road. Being so near the home of our eminent fellow-citizen, U. S. G., at Galena, while my better-half was consuming time among her friends, what could I do better than run over and see friend Ulysses? So we took a run thither, and, having a pleasant chat with Sister Grant at their pleasant home, perched upon an eminence on the south side of the river, we left the company of this cordial, frank, and I should say accomplished lady, and took after Ulysses, who had gone down into the city to smoke his cigar with his old chums on the street. Mrs. Grant gave me the name of General Rowley, at whose office I would be likely to meet her husband. General Rowley informed me that he himself was the only living member of Grant's staff during the war, and that he had come home not long before the close of the war not expecting to live. General Rowley was polite enough to go on to the street and find his illustrious chief and bring him in, and for two hours we three sat and conversed without interruption in General Rowley's office. Much of this conversation ran upon the governments, countries, and peoples, whom the ex-President had visited in his late circuit of the earth. He particularly took up the Turkish Government, and went over with great perspicuity its internal systems of military and civil affairs. He showed himself entirely conversant with its abominable system of taxation, and declared that the Government itself ought not to exist, and that the great Christian Powers, instead of sitting in deliberation of plans for its continuance, should have rather debated measures for its annihilation, subdivision and distribution—making Constantinople a free city. That he has been a sharp, close student of the condition and state of the nations that he has visited was manifest from this conversation. I have on two former occasions come into personal conversation with and observation of Gen. Grant, and have each time been impressed with his directness, simplicity and candor, and never more so than on this occasion. Not one of my neighbors, or intimate friends, would have entered into conversation of the protracted character of this, with less sense of personal consequence, than marked the manners of this distinguished man on this occasion. He seems in superb health and freshness. He said he would come to Milwaukee in June. In speaking of the Presidency he said, "Take any good man but me."

I am persuaded his true position is this: "If my countrymen call me to national service, I will serve them; if not, it is just as well." Now if, as has of late been given out, the South will unite upon this man better than any other, and, as his past record makes him safe on the finance question, then let us lay aside our preferences and unite on him again, that a united people and prosperous land may be its outcome.

We pause next at Moline, and enjoy the hospitality of one of our late Mexican fellow-travelers, at the elegant mansion of his daughter, Mrs. Charles Deer. John Deer, the father of Charles, came from Vermont, and settled at an early day at Grand de Tour, on the Rock River, as a blacksmith, and made plows by hand, using cast-off mill-saws for the mould board of the huge breaking plows of the prairie. He gained a local fame in this direction, and his business became too great for the ordinary shop and he removed to Moline, and started his plow factory on a large scale upon the water-power there. It has grown into an immense establishment—making over one hundred thousand plows per annum and employing five hundred men. Never have I been through an establishment where order, steady industry and marked intelligence was more manifest than here, a place for everything and everything in its place. The father is now aged, a noble Christian man, and, although seventy-five years old, active and useful in all good works. His son inherits all his father's parts and is a grand conductor of a great and useful industry.

What a ride is that from Davenport to Kansas City! It is done from daylight till a little after dark. But what a magnificent country! What a great number of fine houses and barns, villages and cities, churches and school-houses, are seen in Iowa! What great golden cribs of corn; what droves of hogs, cattle, sheep and horses; yea! what a land of plenty and abundance. Its people should be thankful and happy. Yes, indeed, there ought to be a public thanksgiving day as often as once in three months instead of once a year.

Kansas moves on to greatness. The Free-State seed sown upon her soil in 1851 brings forth glorious fruit. Her prosperous and beautiful cities and towns, her schools and churches, her sweet homes, the intelligence and culture of her citizens attest her high character and consequence in the scale of civilization. In population she is talking about a million, for her count in the coming census. At her elections next fall she will vote upon an amendment to her constitution, by which the manufacture and sale of intoxicating drinks are to be prohibited throughout the State. From the speeches of people upon all hands, this amendment to the constitution is to be carried affirmatively. What a crown of glory will this be to a State! Thousands of the best people of all lands will flock to her borders to find deliverance from the curse and crime of intemperance. But what is more, think of the security which her own sons and daughters will find in the bulwark of defense set up in this constitutional provision.

I had the pleasure of meeting Governor St. John. He is a gentleman of the size and general appearance of our Gov. Smith. He commands the confidence of his people much as even Gov. Smith does ours. In conversing with him, upon the exodus of the colored people, he remarked that those who had come to Kansas, as a whole, were getting a living, and that the transfer of the freedmen at the South to the North had but just begun, that their knowledge of their rights and opportunities in this direction was universal throughout all their circles in the South.

The prospects of Kansas seem to be of the most flattering kind at the present time. Our journey through her length, via the Atchison, Topeka & Santa Fe Railroad, was superb; good cars, good track, good eating-houses and polite conductors.

I have come to this place to view this wonder of nature, the Grand Canon of Arkansas. But a dense fog had settled in and upon the mountains, and so I must keep house, and thus it is that you get this letter. Before leaving Colorado I may say something of it.

E. D. H.

LETTER II.

Through Colorado and New Mexico—Old Friends Found in the
Far West—The Grand Canon of the Arkansas.

TRINIDAD, Col., December 19, 1879.

I did not intend when I left home to be lingering so long as I am likely to be upon this side of the Rocky Mountains. But once here, one may as well make what observations he wishes, and be done with it. I am on my way to Santa Fe, and am detained in this semi-Mexican town of 2,500 inhabitants for the train leaving in the evening. Our railroad school in Wisconsin, with Brodhead, Spencer and Merrill as principals, has turned out some pretty good scholars. Such proves to be Wm. S. Strong, who, when I first knew him, was station agent at Janesville. He is now the Vice-President and Manager of the Atchison, Topeka & Santa Fe Railway Company, which, with its branches, has now nigh upon one thousand miles of road running, and is pushing on into New Mexico and Arizona, and thence to the Pacific at San Diego or some other point. Starting from Kansas City (as well as at Atchison) it passes southwesterly for two hundred miles until it reaches the Arkansas River, when it runs along the valley of that river almost due west upon the thirty-eighth degree of latitude until it reaches Pueblo, just in front of the mountains, a distance from the Missouri River of more than six hundred miles. At this point it strikes the Denver and Rio Grande Road, which runs at right angles with it. It starts at Kansas City with an elevation of 600 feet and lands at Pueblo, with 4,700 feet. We knew generally that there was a gradual ascent up these Western plains, and had supposed that this fact would dissipate much of the grandeur of the Rocky Mountains. But not so. The mountains rise from the plain in great glory and beauty. Pike's Peak, the king of the range, is seen lifting his white head high above his fellows for a wide distance around. The Rocky Mountains run nearly north and south. I have now gone along their east front for over a hundred miles along the edge of the plain, and just in front of the mountains. Many of these rise 3,000, 4,000, 5,000, 6,000, and Pike's Peak 10,000 feet from the plain, and are singularly picturesque and beautiful; especially when seen under the light of the morning sun. The range is continuous and interlocked.

The Denver & Pacific Road, leaving the Union Pacific at Cheyenne, runs due south along the front of the mountains to Denver, where the Denver & Rio Grande takes up the line, and continues due south to this place. From this point (which is ten or twelve miles north of the New Mexican line) the Denver and Rio Grande blends with the Atchison, Topeka & Santa Fe Road in its southward course, which it continues for nearly two hundred miles, when it turns west into New Mexico. Thus the main trunk of the Santa Fe Road, from Kansas City to Pueblo, a distance of 600 miles, runs over a level country and is met by lines of road running for 500 miles from north to south at the base of the Rocky Mountains, making the figure of a well proportioned letter T.

Four or five spurs from the top of the letter T—or, from this north and south road, have penetrated the mountains, a distance each of from twenty to fifty miles. Conspicuously among these is that one which runs from Pueblo to Canon City, and thence through the Grand Canon of the Arkansas a distance of some seventy miles in the direction of wonderful Leadville. From this glance at the railroad system of Kansas and Colorado, reaching in all more than a thousand miles, of which the Atchison, Topeka & Santa Fe corporation constitute the head and front, your readers will gather some idea of the marvelous progress which seven or eight short years have wrought in this direction.

Col. Ellsworth, Receiver of the Denver & Rio Grande Railroad, with the consent of the Santa Fe Company (for there is a great quarrel between these two companies), was kind enough to send a special train to take us up through the Grand Canon of the Arkansas. I have seen in my life time a good deal of mountain scenery, but never anything quite so grand and awful as this. For some eight miles perpendicular precipices rise from 1,500 to 2,500 feet on either side, from a narrow gorge, through which the Arkansas River rushes and dashes with great violence. Into this cavern, in some spots, the sun never shines, and the road is cut along the cliff and hangs upon its side. You think, as you pass on, the very mountains, in all their terribleness, are to shut in and crush you. It is quite beyond my powers to describe this display of the Creator's mighty works. You must send out some of your poetic and deft pencil shovers to secure to your readers any fair idea of this wonder of the world.

This quarrel between the Denver, Rio Grande and Santa Fe is now in the Courts, and it is expected will be settled in a short period—when, whichever party is put in possession, the road to Leadville, via this Grand Canon of the Arkansas, a distance from Pueblo of 166 miles, will be speedily completed.

Thirty thousand inhabitants at Leadville, which stands 10,200 feet up in the mountains, and whose existence dates no more than three years back! Think of that.

To-night I will go down on the Santa Fe Road to a place called Los Vegas, and then take stage to Santa Fe, reaching there to-morrow evening.
E. D. H.

Los Vegas, December 20, 1880.

I dropped you a hasty line yesterday from Trinidad, the last town of any consequence in Colorado before entering New Mexico. Trinidad is a busy town of 2,000 inhabitants, with an excellent hotel kept by a Connecticut man. It has a Presbyterian church, and the town is supplied with water works and gas. A small stream runs through the town with power for turning a grist mill. In doing a little shopping I looked into many stores of very considerable stocks of goods. Among these merchants were Messrs. Forbes & Bridge, from Berlin, Wis. Here we found numerous Mexicans. Trinidad is the home of many wealthy ranchmen whose cattle by thousands range upon the wide-spreading and desolate plains around. Hence a good deal of trade with this class of consumers. Mr. Forbes told me his trade was good, and that it was not an unfrequent occurrence to sell one of these ranchmen a bill of $1,000 cash down for his outfit.

Leaving Trinidad we rode all night to reach this place, a distance of 150 miles, arriving at 5 a. m., we remain for the construction train that leaves at 1:30 p. m., and reaching a point twenty-five miles from Santa Fe, stages are in readiness and passengers reach the latter place at 10 p. m.

This place of Los Vegas claims 7,000 people. The streets are full of Mexican ox teams. I noticed two, with three yoke of cattle on each wagon, heavily laden with wool. We have left the cattle ranches of the north and here find the country grazed largely by sheep, so that wool is gathered at this point in large quantities. There are two parts, or sides to this town, divided by a small stream called in English "Chicken Creek," and which is a tributary of the Rio Grande. The east side is the new Yankee town, and the west is the old Spanish town. The former is built of new fresh wood or brick, while the other is made of stone and adobe. The old part of the town looked the strongest and best. Passing one good-looking store which displayed the name of L. Blanchard, in the old town, I said "he is a Yankee sure, though he is here among the Spanish." On entering and inquiring for the proprietor, he was found sitting in his well-furnished parlor in the rear of his store, a dark-complexioned, fine-looking man, and instead of being a Yankee from Massachusetts, he proved to be a Montreal Frenchman, who had lived in New Mexico seventeen years, having driven an ox team from Kansas City over the plains a distance of more than 800 miles. He is now a wealthy and highly respected citizen of this place.

My landlord is a Mr. Jewett, and claims to be distantly connected with Professor Jewett, of Milwaukee. He has a new hotel with forty rooms, costing him $11,000. He too has been in Colorado and New Mexico seventeen years. He and the Yankee set want the tide of emigration to pour in. Blanchard and the Mexican school want no new comers—they want things left as they are.

The day is pleasant and bright, but the wind blows and the dust flies in clouds, and penetrates every crevice. As one man said, the dust will blow through a tin canister. Give me snow, rain and mud rather than this wind and dust.

The man who drove me yesterday from El Moro to Trinidad, a distance of five miles, was a Mr. Cutler, formerly resident at Whitewater. The man who runs stages from where I will get off the railroad into Santa Fe is a Mr. Parker, formerly a conductor upon the old Prairie du Chien road; so you see Wisconsin men take a hand in the occupation of this new strange land.

E. D. H.

LETTER III.

Life in Colorado—The Chances for Fortunes in the Mines—Mining and Farming—Old Milwaukee Settlers.

CHEYENNE, Wyoming Terr., Jan. 1, 1880.

We arrived here an hour ago—having had a delightful ride this bright New Year's morning from Golden in Colorado, a distance of about one hundred and twenty miles. On our right the desert plains stretched out like the billowy ocean to the East. Upon our left the snow-clad mountains stood in august array to the West. Monarch among them all was Long's Peak, 14,271 feet above the sea. There is no snow upon the plains and little upon the lower mountains. We are now back upon our line of travel to the Pacific after a much longer wandering over the plains and among the mountains than we originally contemplated. It had been my intention to have offered you a sketch or two before this, but the journey was so pressing, and having to contend with a bad cold for the last ten days the attempt was postponed, and as we lay over until to-morrow if any thing is said it must be now or not at all. From here to Santa Fe, New Mexico, is five hundred and fifty miles almost due south. A railroad runs from here to within twenty-five miles of that place, and the connection will be made by February 1, next. Just you and your readers stop and think of that for a moment! Five hundred and fifty miles of railroad sweeping from the apex of the great plain land of the continent along the front of the magnificent range of the Rocky Mountains which rise with abruptness and grandeur from the plain for nearly the entire distance. The State of Colorado embraces seven degrees of longitude, to-wit: from the one hundred and second to the one hundredth and ninth—and four degrees of latitude, to-wit: from the thirty-seventh to the forty-first—a very symmetrical boundary, and making her one of the largest States in the Union. If my recollection serves me, Wisconsin has 57,000 square miles of territory. This area will give Colorado over 100,000 square miles. Now this railroad I have named runs but little east of the center of the State, leaving the east half of her territory composed of desert plains and her west half of rugged mountains.

The principal towns and cities of Colorado are situated upon this railroad. They are, beginning at the south, Trinidad, a bright, smart place of 4,000 people; Pueblo, with 6,000 and large expectation, but too much beer and whisky; Colorado Springs, 6,000, beautiful for situation, not a drinking saloon in her midst, schools, churches, newspapers, and a refined population. Denver, the beautiful, 30,000, the seat of wealth and elegance. No city in the land of her size will surpass her in those particulars. There are many other minor places, saying nothing of Leadville, the wonderful, with 30,000 inhabitants. But in these cities of the plain are met the representatives of the two great interests of this great State, viz., ranching and mining. To the consideration of *these* two questions will the traveler in Colorado have his attention continually drawn. One is meeting with intensely interesting characters in this wild exciting Colorado life. In my journey to Santa Fe I was riding in a caboose car, with the construction train, crowded with the roughest of men together with a less number of well-dressed persons. Next me sat a tall well-made man in his prime. He was dressed in the roughest manner. I had noticed him take off and lay at his feet his belt containing a sheath knife and large revolver. We were sitting on benches running lengthwise and much crowded, and consequently must maintain friendly relations. I noticed a bloody wound on the back of this man's hand and said to him: "Sir, I notice you have hurt your hand, and if you will remove the blood I will cover it with a plaster which will give you relief." His courteous and polite answer struck me. This little act, not only afforded an introduction but our acquaintance grew apace. The outcome of it was that I found him a ranchman. He had been thirteen years on the plains, engaged in this business and had met with reasonable success, had come from Illinois and was a graduate of Beloit College, and now, having learned the fact, I had come to the secret of the cultured and refined speech of this coarsely clad and rough exteriored man. He had gone from college to the plains; had encountered all the perils, discomforts and hardships incident to this calling. What has he gained? A few thousand dollars and coarse bread for food and the ground to sleep on at night or perhaps a dug-out or an adobe hut. No wife, no children, no home. He was hearty in health and cheery in spirit to be sure, but to my comprehension, this man, with his outfit in education and manly strength, could have done better. I have fallen in with and have had long interviews with a good many of this class of persons. It is but fair to say that the majority seem to have met with pecuniary success in this calling. A man possessed with two thousand head of cattle takes up small pieces of land along the water courses (which are very few, small and far between) and then claims all the surrounding country. One of these ranchmen told me he wanted fifteen miles square to run his herd of 2,000 head upon, another in New Mexico said for such a herd he occupied eighteen miles square. It is likely that no such quantity of land may be absolutely needed for the maintenance of this number of animals, still, say what they may, it is a barren land and wide districts of it are necessary to provide for a comparatively small number of animals. Water is so scarce that it is probable that the owners of the watering places will for a long time possess the wide pasturage around without interference, and without any title other than a sort of possessory one. But what a life! A few cow-boys, as they are called, upon their ponies follow these herds. By the stream, or at the watering place, there is a hovel and corrall, and yarding facilities of the rudest kind. One ranchman told me that his nearest neighbor was seven miles away. Of course where this system prevails the local church and school are out of the question and as a consequence a low order of civilization must obtain. The graduate of Beloit College for a time may do something to counteract this tendency, but in time it will carry him downward. True the prosperous and wealthy ranchman will bring his family to the "town" and live there, and so it comes to pass that a very considerable portion of the population of the villages and cities is made up of the "lords of the manor" and their families, but what of the cowherds and their wives and children out in the wilderness in their desolate huts, with nothing to ennoble or lift up around them? I can advise no Wisconsin man to leave our fertile fields with all their commercial advantages to exchange them for the ranch life of these desolate plains.

In all this length of mountain range (by which, and into which, my journey has taken me) it has been, ever since the great Pike's Peak excitement (when thousands upon thousands flocked over these plains) as if great flaming trumpeters had stood upon their tops with golden and silver trumpets, and lifting them high so that their voice would penetrate to all lands, proclaiming "Come! Come! Come!—for lo! upon every mountain top and along every valley, and in every dashing river, behold the precious metals, which, when once possessed, every man upon the face of the earth will give of his industry in exchange; ho! come! come! come! And straightway men from all lands have left anvil, plow, jack-plane, briefs, pills, yard-sticks, and even pulpits, and pressing over sea and land have entered these mountains, to smite them, and bore them, and cleave them on every hand that these "hid treasures" should come forth.

Oh! what mavels of muscle, of nerve, of fortitude, of endurance, of patience, of intellect has been, and is being put forth in this great mountain labratory.

It is this grand army of gold and silver hunters thronging this stronghold of what men think is of most material value, viz: the precious metals, that has authorized the construction of this system of railroads out to these mountains, and up and down before them, and into them.

The agricultural interests are spoken of by the citizen as of consequence. But they seem to me small by the side of this vast interest. But is it true, what these trumpeters on the mountain tops with their flaming trumpets proclaim? Ah! there's the rub. Is it true? As I walked up and down the platform at Pueblo, there stood a man by his dog and gun, very coarsely dressed, and grimy and soiled. Supposing him to be a miner, I asked him if he was. He answered in the affirmative.

"How long have you been at work in the mines?"

"Myself and two sons have been at work for three years."

"And have you met with any success?"

"I have just received my first money."

"How much pray?"

"Four hundred dollars."

"Then you have at last found mineral, and this is a product of an actual sale?"

"Yes, sir; and I am now offered ten thousand dollars for a third interest in my mine."

This man, then, who was but a plain man, and who with his boys was supported by his wife's keeping boarders while father and sons toiled in the mountains, were at length abundantly rewarded.

Again. I was riding from Pueblo to Canon City. Across the aisle sat a man below middle life, strong and sturdy. He too was coarsely clothed and grimy with toil. With him I entered into conversation. He told me that he came from England with his father, who was a mining engineer, twenty years ago—that for all that long time he had toiled and labored in search of treasure, and had hardly obtained enough for his daily bread. Indeed he had just now been obliged to send his wife and child to her friends in Kansas, as his means were too scanty for their comfort in the mountains. He in turn asked me where I lived and what sort of a country Wisconsin was. And when I told him it was a fertile land where every one hundred and sixty acres made a beautiful home, and that one home succeeded another for whole towns and counties throughout the State, and that the outcome of such homes was good highways, schools, churches, villages—good laws, and the highest social, intellectual and religious condition, the man was deeply affected at the picture, and said that he had often told his wife that if fortune ever gave them favor they would flee to a paradise like this.

You are told at Denver that it is but three years since Lieut. Gov. Tabor, of Colorado, was but a small merchant at some mountain camp in the mountains—that he made investment in mining stocks and that now he is worth five millions. See how these trumpeters on the mountain tops grow red in the face as they blare this forth to the world. It goes re-echoing along through every city in the land. It spans the seas and awakens man's cupidity far and near, and the thronging crowd moves on.

The old settlers of Milwaukee will remember William Hayward, who kept the gunsmith shop on West Water street. He was a most upright and excellent citizen, and removed to this country many years ago. Between him and myself there existed a cordial friendship when he resided among us. And I was very glad to find him and his excellent wife at Georgetown, whither we came on our journey. This little city, nestled 8,000 feet up in the mountains, is the center of a large and prosperous silver mining interest. Mr. Hayward has been a constant laborer and explorer in these mountains all these toiling years. He brought intelligence, muscle, skill, justice, fortitude and perseverance with him. He has been met by treachery, injustice and oppression beyond what most men can endure. But in the end I am happy to know that a competency has come to him for his declining years. Not as much as he would have had if he had remained in Milwaukee, but oh, what days and weeks and months and years of toil he has put forth, hid away in the clefts of these mountains, that he might bring forth their treasures.

I asked Mr. Hayward what in his judgment would be the daily wages if all the gold and silver that had been taken out of the mountains had been equally distributed among the toilers in the mountains, and he replied that it would not reach seventy-five cents a day. Here is about where the mining business will land. There will be one Tabor in each one hundred thousand who make the venture. There will be one like the man with his two boys who worked three years and was offered $10,000 for a third of their mine, in each ten thousand. There will be quite a large number of men who work for wages who will come out with good savings. But there remain the far larger number who, like the poor Englishmen at the end of twenty years' of toil, have nothing to show, while thousands upon thousands have fallen by the way and lie hid away among the mountains with no sign to mark where they rest. Of these the trumpeters upon the mountain tops say nothing.

How bright and beautiful was the day as we mounted our horses at Farwell's Reduction Works, to ascend the higher mountains under the escort of Mr. Hayward, that we might enter some of these mines and see with our own eyes these achievements of man in finding out the secret places were the great Creator had hid away the precious metals.

We passed the Equator mine, in which some of our Milwaukee people are interested. The foreman being away we did not enter, and, pursuing our journey, ascended to the Coulter, one of Mr. Hayward's discoveries, and upon which he labored seven years before realizing any profit. It is now paying—though he has sold out. Into this we entered, and, each with candle in hand, wound our way far to the depths of the mountain. My little grandson, who rode behind me strapped to my back as we ascended the mountain, was a little timid, but he soon took on courage, plodded his way with candle in hand, and did as well as the rest. At length we reached the "lode," and here the workmen were at work. Mrs. Holton took the pick and with her own hands smote the rock and secured a specimen of the ore in the Coulter mine.

Colorado and New Mexico will for all time beckon the world to come to them for health considerations.

But enough. To-morrow we visit awhile with Governor and Mrs. Hoyt, and then, ho! for Salt Lake.

It will be noted that Wisconsin has furnished a good deal of timber for Governors—Pitkin for Colorado, and Hoyt for Wyoming.

E. D. H.

LETTER IV.

Among the Mormons—Salt Lake City—The Tabernacle—Sunday Services—The Personnel of the Leading Saints—Interviews with the Leaders of the Mormon Church.

SALT LAKE, January 5, 1880.

So far as meeting our Mormon brethren, nothing could have been more opportune. Everybody knows about the **Great Tabernacle**. It seats twelve thousand people. It is an oblong. Its exterior seen at a distance looks like an immense turtle, and it is rough and coarse upon the outside. It is made entirely of wood. Its interior is worthy of careful observation. The immense ceiling springs to its center, supported only by the outside walls. A gallery thirty feet deep resting on pillars, runs along the two sides and front end of the building, while at the west end rise successively three platforms upon which, on the great occasions of public service, sit the various orders of the Priesthood. The upper seat is occupied by the Apostolic Council, chief of which was Brigham Young in his lifetime, now John Taylor. Behind these altars stands the grand organ, one of the largest in the world. A bright, sprightly Englishman is the janitor, who accompanied us to visit the building. He sent us to the extreme east end of the gallery while he stood by the organ in the west end. And now we talked in a whisper, standing 250 feet apart, and could hear each other perfectly. He dropped a pin and its fall was heard as if close by. In like manner could the touch of the hand as it felt along the floor in search of the pin be distinctly heard.

I asked the janitor if he could sing. He replied affirmatively, and drawing his hymn book from his pocket proceeded to the pulpit, where the late Brigham poured forth with stentorian voice, command and exhortation to the Mormon Church, and sung with considerable sweetness one of Zion's songs. The accoustic properties of the vast building seem to be perfect.

But this building is not used by the Saints for public service in the winter, since there is no means of heating it, and Brigham had said that because it was built of wood it would not be safe to attempt to introduce stoves and furnaces. Hence the brethren had no large commodious place in which to hold winter meetings. Accordingly visitors to Salt Lake in the winter would have no opportuniiy of seeing the Saints in any large number together. But it happened, that a new building standing in the same enclosure with the Tabernacle was so far completed as to be used for a State conference—and this conference began its session the evening of our arrival and continued it through yesterday (Sunday).

All the magnates of the church were present and a large concourse equal to five thoustnd people filled to overflowing this new and commodious building. Here then, was our opporunity to worship with the true and genuine Latter Day Saints. In the morning we sallied forth over the crisp snow—for valley and mountain have on white robes—and made our way to the great square enclosed with a high wall, wherein stands the Tabernacle and the temple in process of building and the new assembly hall. Thither the people were flocking and we with them. Already the house was filled. But we pushed into the gallery and found a venerable man with flowing white beard and white hair occupying the chief seat of the Elders, already preaching. This proved to be the celebrated Orson Pratt, now one of the Council of Twelve, and one of the oldest and ablest defenders of the faith.

Brother Orson was enforcing the importance of keeping the "Word of Wisdom." A good deal of diphtheria has prevailed among the Mormon families, and he declared it to be a visitation of God because the heads of families had grown slack in the matter of keeping the " Word of Wisdom."

Upon inquiry I learned that this "Word of Wisdom" was a book of directions as to living, which prohibited all intoxicating drinks, all use of tobacco, tea and coffee. Not a bad book, indeed. Orson admitted that he himself had gone a little astray, but would repent and turn unto the Lord with full purpose of heart, and exhorted all his brethren to do the same, yea, commanded them, if they would turn away the anger of the Most High.

We could not stay through the morning service, for we must go to our own people, and went and found a pleasant house, and (in the contrast) a delightful congregation. Rev. Mr. Barrows, a young and talented man, is the pastor of the Congregational Church, and most heartily did we enjoy that truly Christian service.

In the afternoon we put out at an early hour from our excellent hotel, "The Continental," to give full heed to the service of our Mormon friends in the new assembly hall. But when we came to the place of the great assembly, we found the thronging multitude pressing in, and following on we found ourselves in a standing crowd with no further ingress. Then we turned and went to the gallery, and there we found the same throng. Well, this would not do. We must have a fair show; we must come near to the chief saints; therefore turning, we made our way through the throng to the very front of the altar and into the front aisle. There stood a decent looking man as usher, and accosting him I said, we were strangers and would thank him for a seat. He secured two good seats for us very near and directly before the rising platforms of the distinguished members of the priesthood elders, bishops, apostles. Behind them all, upon the upper platform, and before the great company of the singers, sat the members of the Council, at the right hand of whom was the venerable President, and successor of the illustrious Brigham, John Taylor.

At the front, and near where we sat, was a long table upon which the Communion Service of bread and water was spread. Before this table sat twelve Bishops to dispense the elements. Among these Bishops was a brother of Brigham, an old man who slept much during the service.

The service began by singing. Bishop Cannon, brother of the delegate at Washington, presided. After singing, one of the

Bishops led in prayer, which would have been a proper one in any Christian assembly; again singing, by the choir of fifty singers, then a blessing on the bread. Now, the elements were distributed by many hands to the great congregation of five thousand people, for the new building is a fine and large one, with gallery the entire circuit. But the preaching must go on contemporaneously with the taking of the communion, and it did.

On this first occasion, when a great congregation of the saints were able to meet in the winter, who should preach if the Head of the Church did not? John Taylor, President of "the Church of Jesus Christ of Latter Day Saints" arose in his chief place and stood forth. He is a man 70 years old, hair and beard white as snow; is nearly six feet high and well proportioned; a large, fine head, his black frock coat well buttoned—and he posed himself as if he was an orator indeed. His speech, slow and measured, was, upon the whole, dull. After complimenting Brother Pratt's address of the morning, and urging that more attention be given to the "Word of Wisdom," he repeated the Lord's prayer and took the words "Thy Kingdom Come" as the foundation of his discourse. There had been many kingdoms of all sorts and sizes, but God's kingdoms among men had been few and far between. But in these latter times a revelation had been made through Joseph Smith that had brought in a new dispensation, the Latter Day Saints. And right here and now in this very church did we not know that we were God's people? Did not these Bishops through whom the Holy Ghost had been communicated to thousands upon thousands by the laying on of hands, did they not know it? Certainly they did, declared this man who spoke by authority. This being so, what became our duty? Clearly to stand in our lots and places as saints should stand. We had enemies. Our holy and divinely established religion was attacked; should we regard God's law or man's law? And rising to great voice and true pathos, he declared that he for one should stand by God's law, and then appealed to the congregation to know its views, to be declared by the uplifted hand. All hands, men, women and children, five thousand strong, were shown affirmatively.

The great man sat down, and then came forward Joseph Smith, Jr., a nephew of the Prophet, also one of the "Council of Twelve," the highest Mormon judicatory. "Yes," said Joseph, "I never expect to be delivered from persecution until the great day of Christ's coming. The wicked world is at emnity with God's saints, always has been and always will be. But His saints must stand and endure hardship as true soldiers, leaving the consequences with God."

Singing, some notices, and a benediction, closed this meeting. The order, quiet and attention of the congregation was exemplary. The average physiognomy of the people was fair. There were no handsome women, and all were dressed plainly but decently.

The Salt Lake *Tribune* of this morning makes Mr. Taylor say the following in his discourse: "I defy the United States. I will obey God; these are my sentiments."

I think the speaker used no such language as his defiance of the United States. His assertion that he would obey God I have already recited, and this was its extent. He might have had an ulterior intent. But still I do not think it fair for the *Tribune* to put such words of treason in his mouth when they were not uttered.

The institution of polygamy is no new thing. It has cursed every nation and age that has practised it. It is a great curse to this people, being founded in sensuality and lust, despite all the special pleading of Orson Pratt and their other thinking and intellectual men. The Government should lay strong hands upon it, and enforce with vigor a law declaring polygamy an offense to good morals and a crime.

We spent yesterday in going among the brethren. We called upon Mr. Eldridge, the manager of the "Zion's Co-operative Mercantile Association," in his magnificent store of 105 feet wide and 316 feet long, three stories above the basement, and in which he sells $4,000,000 worth of goods per annum. Mr. Eldridge politely went with us from end to end of his extensive establishment. Every kind of merchandise is kept in full stock. Mr. Eldridge is a man of 55 years of age, a sober, sensible and candid man, the husband of four wives.

From Brother Eldridge we went to pay our respects to Brother Taylor. We found him in Brigham's old office, a small yellow building standing next to Brigham's dwelling, and where he died. Taylor only keeps his office here, his residence being away in another part of the city. Taylor is not a rich man, and only has four wives. Brigham was pretty heavy on the wife business—the number was above twenty. We found Mr. Taylor in conversation with two or three gentlemen. His secretary handed him my letter from Gov. Smith, which at once commanded his attention, and, dismissing the gentlemen present, gave my wife and myself a most courteous and polite audience, continuing it as long as we chose to remain. He is a gentleman in manners, has a strong, benevolent, and I may say handsome face, is an Englishman by birth, coming out through Canada. He seems to command, upon the whole, the confidence of his people. But he is without the strong, magnetic, organizing force which Brigham possessed.

The balance of the day was employed in sleighriding through and around the beautifully located, and, in some respects, the beautifully built city of Salt Lake.

The mountains stand in glorious array around, shutting it on every hand, save towards the north. We are here at Ogden, now, and in two hours will resume our journey westward. E. D. H.

LETTER V.

Musings on the Way—The Great American Desert—The Sierra Nevadas—Sacramento Valley—Arrival in the City of the Golden Gate.

SAN FRANCISCO, Jan. 13, 1880.

If it were not irreverent I would almost ask the Creator if He really thought He was doing a good work when He made all that piece of the continent lying between the upper waters of the Platte and the upper waters of the Sacramento. I can fancy that He might reply to such a challenge as this, by saying that He began the making of the United States on the eastern side with a large assortment of good material; that He made the New England States of good stuff; that He put into New York, New Jersey and Pennsylvania a superior quality of material; put pretty good stuff into all the States south of the Blue Ridge and the Ohio River, and then came to making Ohio, Indiana, Michigan, Illinois, Missouri, Iowa and Minnesota. These used up a very large amount of the stuff that goes to make up the best elements for man's sustenance and happiness. But when He came to make Wisconsin he was so lavish in the use of the best elements of earth's highest estate that the material left on hand was very poor and refuse, and He just piled it up between the two water courses named, serving a sort of usefulness in holding the two sides of the country together, and that's about all.

It was night when we entered the cars to pursue our journey from Ogden. Two nights and two days have been heretofore employed to measure the 882 miles from Ogden to San Francisco. Your readers may not all keep in mind that what we call the Central Pacific Railroad is composed of two distinct corporations, namely, the Union Pacific from Omaha to Ogden, 1032 miles, and the Central Pacific from Ogden to San Francisco, 882 miles—total 1914 miles. We slept well that night from Ogden. The road was smooth, and the cars were of superior make. The morning dawn brought the interminable desert, more drear now if possible than in Wyoming. For all the day we were passing along the Humboldt river. To be sure in many places, along a narrow skirt of meadow would be seen cattle feeding upon its grass, but mostly alkali land, with only sage brush, prevailed. Mountains are always in sight, sometimes far away and sometimes near at hand, but always stark and naked of verdure or trees. At suitable distances, upon the whole line, excellent eating places with hotel accommodations have been established—and around these places, in some instances, are considerable villages. Large herds of cattle are, after all, sustained upon these dismal plains in wide ranges and their owners go to make up population, and produce business, in these villages. Mining also obtains in all this wide expanse of intermingled mountain country.

Conspicuous among the verdant spots in this desert land, is the Humboldt Station. Its owners antedated the railroad, and commanded a stream of pure water, descending from the mountains, at no distant point from the depot. They were so generous with the company that it in turn makes it a stopping and eating place for all trains. And these owners use their mountain stream not only to supply the engines and travelers, but they have made fountains and irrigating channels and planted trees and created lawns so that a beautiful specimen is given of what may be done in the desert with water. As the night came on we came to the Sink of the Humboldt river—where this considerable river is lost in the desert sands. Sometimes it is quite a lake, but now it would appear from what I could see as we passed it on the cars, but a wide reedy marsh.

This is the last night in the great journey. As it shuts in, the clouds lower and the wind assumes a mournful dirge-like sound, as it soughes with terrific force around the train. The snow commences to fall. But we speed on our way. We are nearing the Sierra Nevada Mountains. We wanted to make this part of the journey by daylight, but cannot. The one passenger train per day allows of no choice, and so we plunge on into the night and down the mountains. The snow was heavy and the storm was fierce and came near detaining our train as it did subsequent ones. But we came on and at daylight the descent was made and we were among the foot-hills of the mountains, with the snow turned to a heavy rain, and in place of sage grass and desolation the beautiful green grass and evergreen trees. As we swept along down the Sacramento Valley and the day advanced, the rain ceased, and the sun came forth revealing a world of splendor and magnificence. It was delightful indeed to come again to a land of homes—sweet fields and all clustering evidences of a prosperous and happy people.

By a cut-off recently made by the Central Pacific, the journey from Sacramento to San Francisco is shortened by some sixty miles and the passenger reaches the latter city some three or four hours sooner than he used to. It was a lovely ride from Sacramento that bright morning—all the hill sides and the wide stretching meadows were lustrous with green. The plowmen were seen afield on every hand. That ride embraced two journeys upon the waters of the glorious bay—one by which a massive boat takes the whole train for a space of five miles, and again when we leave the train at Oakland, to pass by ferry boat to the City of the Golden Gate. Here we found admirable quarters in one of her great hotels at noon of Thursday, the 8th of January, having had a most prosperous journey from the Great Lakes to the wondrous Pacific Coast.

I may not conclude this letter without an observation or two about the Pacific Railroad. Whatever poor material the Lord may have had to make up the country over which the national highway runs, considering so much was put into mountains, it is just splendid to witness how they were set aside and a passage way left for this road to come through. A great share of the road was very cheaply made. That is, made without large cost. It is a well constructed road in all particulars. The train upon which we came was composed of one express car, one baggage car, one emigrant and smoking car, one day car and one sleeper. There were not more than twenty-five passengers all told. So far as this one train would show, the business would seem small. The conductors and station-keepers spoke of the westward bound trains as running very light this winter. Costly as was this road and large as was the national contribution to it, and rich as are the men who derived those large subsidies for building a road not so very costly, yet it is all right. I regard Mr. Oakes Ames as an injured man. Few men of capital were willing to grapple at the time with this work. The books of subscription for taking stock in this road were left with me for the entire State of Wisconsin, and after public advertisement there was but one man to be found in the State that would subscribe for a dollar—he took five thousand dollars. That gentleman was Mr. Thompson, of Racine, former Manager of the Western Union Railroad. For months the project lay open and none of the great capitalists of the country would touch it.

Oakes Ames, a tough, strong, self-made man, bred to making shovels, now with his large wealth stepped into the arena and called around him men equally brave and tackeled the east end of the road. Huntington, Stanford, Crocker and Hopkins, up here at Sacramento—country merchants—but possessed of the real Yankee grit, tackeled the west end. Great indeed were the difficulties to be overcome. The cutting through the mountains was not the greatest. Think of drawing drinking water forty miles for man and beast engaged in the work of construction! The *horror-*

ableness of the desert was enough to appal most men. But these two sets of men pushed through the work and the Government *settled* with them, and then did the unspeakable mean thing of turning upon these men, conspicuously Mr. Ames, and pursuing him to his grave with every sort of vile, but unproved, accusation. This subsidy to the Pacific Railroad was justified much as were many of the war measures—from the necessity of the case.

But now let it be the very last ever to be granted by the Federal Govervment. First, for the reason that it has no constitutional right to grant any whatever ; second, that it has no capacity to conduct them if it had the power to grant them. E. D. H.

LETTER VI.

On the Pacific Coast—Topographical Picture of San Francisco—
Its Banks—Its People—Its Sea-Side Resorts—Sea Lions.

SAN FRANCISCO, Cal., Jan. 20, 1880.

We made our advent to the Golden State amid wind, snow and rain. But as we came to the lowlands the storm subsided, the clouds lifted, the sun came forth, and all was luminous and bright at midday, and nature's welcome was cordial and gladsome. At night, however, the clouds came on and all was sour and dark. The second day brought a cold, heavy rain, and but little could be done in the way of going forth. Under the escort of Mr. P. C. Cole, so well known in Milwaukee, we visited the Bank of California, where I found an old personal friend in the cashier, Mr. B. Murray, formerly cashier, or rather assistant cashier, in the American Exchange Bank of New York. Most cordial was my welcome at the hands of this accomplished gentleman and bank officer. We visited the Exchange, where Bulls and Bears do congregate and make hideous roaring betimes; also the Woman's Exchange, for the women here are stock brokers and dealers as well. We visit d the costly "Turkish bath" built by Senator Jones—but not any better, if as good as the Milwaukee baths, for practical purposes. My wife has since taken a bath there, and thinks it not as good. We visited the famous safety vaults—the same as the First National Bank has, and the same as Mr. Mitchell has constructed in his building. But these are on a very extended scale, larger, Mr. Cole says, than any in the United States elsewhere. We visited Mr. Andrew's jewelry store called the Diamond Store, the very ceiling of which is studded with genuine diamonds. Andrews began his career as a sidewalk hawker of cheap jewelry. All this tramping I did under an umbrella with my pantaloons turned up at the bottom. It was enough for the first day and a fair beginning. Everybody was scolding the weather and declaring it unprecedentedly cold. I had expected to have found my neighbor and friend, Col. Yates, here, but instead, a letter from San Diego saying that he had found the weather so cold and bad here that he was obliged to flee, and was now at San Diego in all glorious summer, and urged us to join him. A leading member of my party now united in this general proclamation against the San Francisco climate, and urged immediate flight. But there come times when all persons in command must put their foot down with firmness. So it devolved upon your humble servant to say whether we should stay or go. In deciding this question, one needs to consider the objects of a journey to this coast. If it be health, and drouth and warmth be the conditions of its promotion and preservation, why then let such hie themselves to the sunny and dry climate of San Diego. But not so with us. We had come to see the people of California, to note their institutions, their buildings, the thousand and one activities by which one generation of men have built up great cities, displaying superb architecture, and unparalleled costliness, opened up highways through the fastnesses of the mountains and bidden the steam horse to go swiftly through and over them; built mighty ships, which but yesterday had no existence, and bidden them to go upon the ocean, hitherto untracked by steam, and open quick trade with the millions on millions of the Asiatic races; a people who have had the courage and nerve to maintain specie payments when the whole nation beside had apostatized and gone after shin plasters, falsely called money; a people who have studied out new problems in State government, and are apparently putting them into successful operation. No, we cannot go summering to San Diego.

If Paris is France, so is San Francisco, California. We must stay here. Climate, in a sense, is of no consequence with well people. As between heat and cold, that is a question of more or less wool. One needs considerable time in a metropolitan city to get ready for work. Familiarity with streets and places, with its geography and topography, are necessary; with its railroad depots and steamboat wharves, with its horse-car and steam-dummy routes; these mastered, each active day's work brings information and pleasure.

The third day after our arrival, came off clear and beautiful, although, as all said, it was cold. But this cold that they talk about is above freezing. Well, what shall be done on this third day? The six-year-old-boy in the party had been told glowing stories about the sea lions, to be seen on the rocks which rise out of the Pacific Ocean, and his voice was raised long and loud, that the first and most important thing to be done was to see the lions and the ocean. To tell the truth, his older fellow travelers participated not a little in the boy's curiosity, so it was decided that we go forth and see these sights. Incidentally the journey affords an opportunity to make a grand observation of the breadth of the city, and upon the heights which are passed a fine view of it and of the bay, the Golden Gate, and the ocean is gained. Let me attempt just a little outline of this city and its surroundings, as some of your readers may not have studied it. A tongue of land comes up from the south between the coast and the bay of San Francisco. This tongue of land has an average width of eight miles from east and west; and a length from south to north of twenty-five miles. On this tongue of land are many abrupt hills and semi-mountains, but at its northeastern terminus is a handsome plateau of land upon which the city is built. The waters of the bay at the northeast corner of this peninsula turn a right angle and continue a wide open water way towards the west for some six miles, with a width of five miles. At this point, the mountains from the north close in the waters of the bay and the ocean, against a rocky shore on the San Francisco side, until the space is but two miles wide. Here at this narrow pass is the Golden Gate proper For two miles further the shores widen, and at once, the mariner is out upon the broad expanse of the Pacific Ocean. This narrow place is particularly and especially the "Golden Gate." A magnificent entrance to a magnificent harbor! This inside waterway is composed of two bays, the Bay of San Francisco and San Pablo Bay. This water-way, which should have had but one name, runs nearly north and south. Its average width is six miles and the two bays will measure more than forty miles from south to north. Deep water prevails over the most of this inland sea. The entrance to the ocean is nearly midway of its length. Beautiful cities and villages line its shores. Directly opposite San Francisco, five miles across the bay and due east, is the city of Oakland, with its 40,000 inhabitants. This is to San Francisco what Brooklyn is to New York. It is a city of churches, fine homes, and a higher grade of people.

Now for the ocean and the sea lions. Come with me from our home in the Grand Hotel on Market street up Montgomery due north four blocks to California street. Here we come to a new and peculiar street railway. It consists of what is called a dummy and an ordinary street railway car. They are attached. The dummy draws the car. The dummy has outside seats running lengthwise of the car. Between the seats are the levers and machinery for propelling the two cars, and there stands the engineer. There is no steam on board. You ask how is this train propelled? Between the track and under ground is a cable running upon rollers for the length of the road, say three miles. Access to this cable is had by a crack running in the center of the track of the width of one inch, through which descends an arm of iron, say eight inches wide and three-fourths of an inch thick, which at the pleasure of the engineer can grasp the revolving, or passing cable, and so have his train carried on as fast as the cable goes. A stationary engine of large power revolves this cable. I have not been to these works as I intend to do, to learn more particularly the facts of this California invention. But we are aboard on California street, and the first dash is made right up a steep hill at as swift a rate as we go down hill or as we go on the level. In passing along this road we go by the palatial homes of the Stanfords', the Hopkins' and the Coltons', and many others. They are upon heights that command land and water for wide distances. But on we go over hill and dale. Plebian homes are in the hollows (which are best off when the wind blows and the sand flies in clouds) and patricians on the mountain tops. Three miles brought us to the end of this superb method of locomotion. Here we come to an omnibus for the remaining four miles to the ocean, a light one drawn by two horses. The young man in charge tells me his horses are good, that he charges twenty-five cents for each passenger, and that he came from the State of Maine. Well, away we go over as fine a macadamized road as you ever drove upon. In this journey we are in the midst of sand mountains. Originally they had no verdure or shrubbery upon them; but now they have been largely appropriated to homes for the dead. Protestant cemeteries, Catholic cemeteries, Jewish cemeteries, and Masonic cemeteries. Trees have been planted and varied artistic floral and horticultural work supplied, so that the desert is redeemed. But ah, see, see! Was it the Spaniard Balboa who in 1523 first set European eyes upon the Pacific Ocean? His gladness was celebrated by religious observances. Well, Neddie, the boy, cried out "Grandpa, there's the ocean," and clapped his litttle hands, and his grandpa lifted his hat at the grand sight, and I guess his grandma thought, if she did not shout, Amen.

Right upon the shore of the ocean stands the Cliff House, an extensive hotel restaurant. It is perched upon the rock, say forty feet from the water. Directly before this house, say five hundred feet away, rise abruptly from the water three conical rocks, naked and bare. The principal one of these rocks I judge rises from the water forty feet. The others perhaps half that height. Their diameter at the water's edge may be thirty to fifty feet, and are perhaps thirty to fifty feet apart from each other. It is upon these rocks that the sea lions have come and made a home. Upon any sunny day hundreds of these monsters may be viewed from the broad porch of this hotel at pleasure. The weight and size of these animals is from one hundred to one thousand pounds. Here they lie upon rocks writhing and crawling over each other. They thrust their long tapering necks and little heads up and cry and howl like dogs, keeping up a terrible din. Ever and anon you will see schools of them playing around in the surging waves that lash the rocks. And now watch this one, as he approaches the rocks, and waits, until he gets a good strong wave to carry him high up the side of the rock where he is landed and begins his crawling, climbing motion to get up among his fellows. His hind flippers act as feet, while his forward ones act as hands and arms to help him on. At length he is in a sunny spot, and there he stretches himself. His hair, still saturated with the sea water, shines like a black glass bottle. But by and by, as he dries, he has a yellowish color.

It is said that each of these creatures on an average consume thirty pounds of fish per day, and the Fish Commissioners for this State have given the opinion that it costs too much to preserve them for mere show purposes, for they are protected by statute.

To see them, as you do on these rocks, with their slow and tedious motion, and apparently inactive and incapable movement, you wonder how they can catch thirty pounds of fish. But go now to Woodward's Garden, one of the show places of the city, and witness the movements of this animal as he is there exhibited. There is but one. He weighs two hundred pounds. He is kept in a pond or reservoir, say fifty feet in diameter. Twice a day he is fed on eight pounds of small fish. An hour before the time of feeding he appears and begins to swim about holding his lithe cat-like head out of the water, continually calling and crying for his food. The man comes at length and plants himself by the railing that surrounds the pond, with his basket of fish. Instantly Mr. Sea Lion is at his side, and now we will observe if he be the stupid, slow-going individual we supposed him to be as he lay creeping and waddling and writhing on the rocks. The man takes a fish, weighing, say half a pound, and throws it clear across the pond. Never did arrow fly swifter than did this monster as he darted for his prey, and seizing it, turned himself and returned with equal velocity to the place of starting, ready for another turn ; and thus it was seen that snail as he was on the rocks, he was lightning in the water, and woe betide the poor fish on whose track the sea lion comes.

The journey to visit the sea lions and the Pacific Ocean was a well-spent day in promoting the objects of a visit to California.

E. D. H.

LETTER VII.

A Visit to the Suburban City of Oakland — Mayor Kalloch and Other Officials — The School System.

OAKLAND, Cal., January 23, 1880.

It is three days since we removed from the great city of 300,000 inhabitants to this lesser one of 40,000. Our home is 855 Washington street, "Clarendon House." We rent a suite of rooms and live at our pleasure, either on the street, like Arabs, or in our own home. There are great inconveniences, to the diligent traveler, at being shut up to the regular meals of hotel life. The "apartment" life is far the best, most economical and convenient. For example, we are invited out, to be guests of a friend for two days and a night. Very well, shut shop and go, leaving all baggage, save your satchel. The rent of my house is, say, one dollar and a half per day, whereas, at any of the principal hotels, my daily expenses would reach six or eight dollars, and no allowance for absences. But I sat down to say something of the municipal affairs of San Francisco.

Yesterday, I set apart, to visit the Mayor of the city, and other public functionaries at the City Hall, which is fully twelve miles from my home in Oakland. But, see how nicely I am circumstanced for going and coming. My house stands on the corner of Washington and Seventh streets. Along Seventh street, trains on the Central Pacific Road of four, five and six, large, long, and elegant paseenger cars, pass both ways, every half hour in the day. Each train stops at my house, so that I can step off, or on, at pleasure, and with the greatest convenience. When you go into a strange place, to see, and be seen, have an eye to its public conveniences. The Central Pacific has several tracks running through Oakland, beside its main overland track. For, all overland passengers approach San Francisco, through Oakland. But a peculiar feature attaches to these splendid trains of cars, continually running through this city. There is no charge to passengers riding in them within the limits of Oakland. For example, I took my little grandson, night before last, to take a free ride to Alameda, two miles away. Off we went, riding by most beautiful homes, gardens, and grounds, laden with green shrubbery and odorous with flowers, and the mighty evergreen oaks, which doubtless gave the town its name. It was the time of the closing of the afternoon schools, and as we made frequent stops, in came bevies of school children, availing themselves of free-riding to get to their homes.

This right of free passage, upon any trains of the road, through Oakland, reserved to its inhabitants, comes, for the right of way, granted to trains, through streets, and for docking, and ferry privileges. But on the ferries a charge is made of fifteen cents each way and from this source doubtless a revenue is derived abundantly compensating for all this free railroad service within the bounds of the city of Oakland.

The day was glorious as we stepped on our train to visit Mr. Kalloch, the Mayor of San Francisco, at the City Hall, twelve miles away. We ran four miles by rail. A portion of that distance, say two miles, is upon piles, getting far out into the bay so as to shorten the ferriage as much as possible. Here we come to the railroad company's extensive docks, and where the ferry is in waiting to take us five miles across the bay. About half a mile from these docks in the direct route to San Francisco is Goat Island, a small mountain, rising abruptly from the water. Your readers will remember that the railroad company wanted the Government to grant them this island for wharf purposes, which it refused to do. It would for many reasons appear that it could have wisely granted this request, giving the company solid and large ground for its wharves, and shortening the passage across the bay by this half mile.

We are off on the ferry. Magnificent, indeed, is this steamship. No teams allowed upon it—all devoted to the thronging hundreds and thousands of passengers. It is 250 or 300 feet long and proportionately wide. The whole lower deck is left for standing and walking room, with some seats, while the upper saloon, superbly upholstered, would seat not less than five hundred people. She moves with the utmost precision, firmness, and strength. The order and neatness is perfection itself—so silent and quietly is every thing done, that you would think it instinct with life. No officers are seen, and but few servants. These are neatly dressed, and as speechless as automatons.

We land at the foot of Market street, the Broadway of San Francisco. Twenty horse cars, more or less, are in waiting, ready to take the passengers over their ramifying tracks to any part of the city. My route leads directly up Market street, two miles or more, to the City Hall.

This is a great, long, straggling establishment, and, in its unfinished condition, looks like a ruin upon its outside. It stands in fact in the "Sand Lots." In other words, the place where "Denis Kearney" and his compatriots do congregate, each Sunday afternoon, is in the open "unkempt" part of the public square, lying upon the south side of the City Hall, a space of land composed of sand—hence "Sand Lots."

Our first respects must be paid to the head of the city and county government, Mayor Kalloch. The Mayor was a Baptist clergyman—a man of eloquence and power, displayed in Boston, in New York, in Kansas, and finally in the Tabernacle, here in San Francisco (a large edifice on Fifth street, near Market), where he so fearlessly discussed public questions, denouncing corporation evils and Chinese dangers, that the attention of the "Sand Lotters" was turned towards him, and he was nominated for Mayor at their instance. DeYoung, of *The Chronicle*, denounced him—and reproduced the old charges of immoral conduct, and at length brought vile accusations against Kalloch's dead father, whereupon Kalloch declared the mother of DeYoung was a prostitute. DeYoung in a dastardly way came upon Kalloch, unawares, and shot him. At first it was supposed that he could not survive the wound. Pending his dangerous illness, the election occurred, and he was triumphantly elected. But he is not well. He has attempted to assume the duties of his office, but the day I was there he was confined to his home, and there is at this time some apprehension that he may not, after all, get well.

Turning from the Mayor's office, we proceeded to the Board of Education, hoping to find the Superintendent of Public Instruction, to the end that at that time, or some other, I might, with him, visit the public schools. But he was not in. His Secretary gave me the Twenty-Sixth Annual Report of the Superintendent of Public Schools, a book of 350 pages, which I send to be placed in *The Sentinel* library.

At a glance at it, it will be seen that 19,926 boys, and 18,203 girls, were the number of enrolled pupils for the last year. Total income of the school department for the year just closed is $856,-107.52. The value of school property in San Francisco is something over $3,000,000. This makes splendid pecuniary showing for a city thirty years old, in the direction of public education.

The Secretary of the Board directed me to the *Lincoln* school as a good specimen. After visiting the City and County Clerk, with whom I had a long interview, and who gave me a copy of the City Reports of 862 pages, I went to this *Lincoln* school, Mr. Edwards, of Gorham, Maine, was its principal. He was so engaged with callers that he sent his head teacher with us, and we visited six of the different class rooms, each containing fifty pupils. In this building were thirteen hundred boys. All was order, decorum and apparent thoroughness. If the truth must be told, one of these class rooms was not duly criticised on account of the beauty and sweet manners of the "school marm." I must not lisp her name; if I did there would be a stampede of young men from the East to the West, and I fear duels would be fought. What I did not know before I learned now, that the boys and girls of San Francisco attend separate schools. This is in violation of the old New England practice and the universal common school practice of our country, and in violation of the best condition and interests of education and the welfare of the sexes. Coeducation of the sexes in schools is as valuable as in the family.

The city and county of San Francisco is governed by one and the same body of men. Twelve Supervisors, representing so many wards, is the legislative body for the city and county, and are elected on a general ticket. While the candidate is to be the resident of a given ward he must be voted for by all the other wards. So it will be seen, that it becomes the interest of each ward to put up its best man, and if the parties do not put up good men it becomes easy for independent organizations to do so. So that in either event, it is reasonably certain that good men are to become Supervisors. They hold their office for two years, and receive a compensation of $1,200 per annum. The Mayor is elected for two years, salary $3,000. The County Clerk receives $4,000, Sheriff $8,000, Auditor $4,000, Treasurer $4,000, Assessor $4,000, Tax Collector $4,000, License Collector $3,000, Register of Voters $3,600, Surveyor $500 and fees, Superintendent of Public Streets $4,000, Coroner $4,000, etc. These will suffice as specimens. The Park Commissioners and Water Commissioners serve without pay.

The real estate of San Francisco for the last year appraised at $191,078,000, and the personal property $52,298,000, and the amount raised for all purposes in the city and county as per Tax Collector's report for 1879, is $5,513,536.08. This seems a large sum to raise for 300,000 people. How does the inventory of property compare per capita with ours, and how does the percentage of tax compare with that of Milwaukee? I have long believed that our dual government of city and county was an evil, and that one should be wiped out, and by so doing a large saving would be made in the annual expenses of the people and their affairs managed a great deal better.

If I write any more I shall fail to meet my engagement to dine with Capt. C., who has agreed to take me to places next March where trout of the first quality and size are to be taken. So as I don't want to lose either my dinner or the chance of taking California trout, I must quit gossiping with you.   E. D. H.

LETTER VIII.

San Francisco—Its Dark Side—Licentiousness and Stock Gambling—Its Bright Side—Christian Churches and Schools.

SAN FRANCISCO, Cal., February 2, 1880.

The sin of licentiousness seems to have been among the most fatal of all the catalogue of evils that came with man's fall. Nothing more degrades the soul, dries up all its better and finer sensibility, or quicker sends the body to be food for worms than this vice.

The Divine Judgment was exemplified in the utter destruction of the Cities of the Plain, where the degradation had become so universal that ten righteous persons could not be found among the entire population.

In all the ages, and along every path which man has trodden, this appalling source of woe has been present. It finds its chief seat and centre in great cities. Perhaps in modern times no city shows it in a bolder and more offensive form than the city of London. Hundreds of women can be met in the gas lights of that city plying their trade in the most open and unblushing manner. In New York, the open display of the evil is not near as offensive as it was years ago, and yet its practice is wide and devastating. Chicago and San Francisco, from common consent, are largely involved in the dire evil, and this leads me to speak of what is reasonably patent upon this subject in this city.

Every city has its grand centre. Market street is to San Francisco what Broadway is to New York. From Market street runs to the north Sansome, Montgomery, Kearney and Dupont streets. On these five streets (including Market) and their immediately adjoining and connecting streets are the fine stores, banks, offices and hotels of the city. Go upon Montgomery or Kearney streets upon any fine afternoon and you will see as many handsome, well-dressed and well-mannered women as can be seen in any city, probably, in the world. I think I have never seen handsomer women than here. This applies to the virtuous woman as well as to those living outside of the pale of virtue.

In this district of the city which I have defined are hundreds of well-furnished suits of apartments on the second, third and fourth floors of spacious and elegant buildings, which are rented out by the week or month I looked into numbers of these attractive places and found those which would have suited me well, and to which I would have liked to have taken my family, but well-informed and discreet friends shook their heads and said No, and I asked why, and the answer, not perhaps quite as plainly spoken as I shall write it here, was that these elegant and attractive places were in too many cases houses of prostitution or assignation.

A young gentleman friend, well versed in the city, kindly accompanied me in one of my searches for "apartments," and he generally warned me away from all this region for the reason given. "Well," said I, "I find this thing is pretty extensive here." "Oh, yes," he replied, "so general that nothing is thought of it. It is no longer regarded as vice." Very well, so thought the inhabitants of those old cities. But neither then, or at any time since, have the consequences of this transgression been stayed. Fine apparel, fine manners, fine equipage, fine apartments, may soothe the conscience and postpone the day for a little, that is all.

It is to be observed that no open intemperance is witnessed in the streets of San Francisco. Nor is any loud brawling and boisterous talk heard. Nor is the practice of stock jobbing and gambling as rampant now as in former days. Still this attracts thousands of men and women to Montgomery, Pine and California streets daily to deal in stocks. This business is largely done in the open street. The elegant Exchange building on Pine street, between Sansome and Montgomery, is the place where the stocks are publicly called and dealt in by the large brokers and dealers. None can enter here but members, and a membership costs $25,000. The transactions here serve to fix the price. But I fancy that a larger business is done outside, by the thousands on the curb stones, than here in the Exchange itself. Let it be remembered that there is no rain to interfere with the standing from morn till eve on the pavement, if you desire to do so. Though this is called the rainy season, there has been but two out of the twenty-six days of my residence here upon which any rain has fallen.

I am not attempting in this random way of writing to analyze the vices of the great city of the Pacific Coast. I have incidentally glanced at one, and her vice of gambling has been, and still is, one that carries its thousands to sorrow and misery.

It will be borne in mind that if old Father Lot could have but found ten righteous in the city it would have been saved.

Let the righteous, then, take courage. The dark spots of London, of New York, of Chicago, and of San Francisco, are shut up and narrowed in, and all without illumed and made full of hope, courage, joy, human happiness and salvation by the individual and collective exercise of the Christian faith.

So here in San Francisco grandly and nobly stand, in the antithesis of all the sins, vices and crimes that any of its guilty inhabitants may practice, a grand company of those who side themselves with the law of religion, as witness the following statistics: In the city are the following named religious organizations under the authority of the sacred Scriptures, viz: six Baptist, five Congregational, nine Episcopalian, six Evangelical Lutheran, six Hebrew Congregations, twelve Methodist, fourteen Presbyterian, fourteen Catholic, two Swedenborgian, one Unitarian, one Universalist and eleven miscellaneous church organizations, besides which are fourteen Bible, Missionary, and Young Men's Christian Associations, and other kindred societies. Making in all one hundred separate organizations, embracing many thousands of the good men, women and children of this important city who, in one form or another, adhere to the faith of Him who spake as never man spake, and who furnish moral and religious salt enough to serve the city and make grand progress in all that conserves human welfare.

E. D. H.

LETTER IX.

The Garden of California—Santa Clara Valley—The Almaden Quicksilver Mines—San Jose—Old Friends.

SAN JOSE, Cal., February 9, 1880.

You don't know Mr. Waters, of San Jose, California, do you? Well, he is a dapper little fellow, and is the livery stable keeper just opposite the Auzarias House, kept by Mr. Churchill, formerly of the United States Hotel in Milwaukee. I waited on Mr. Waters to learn if he could furnish me with a team and carriage sufficient to transport eight persons, great and small, from the city of San Jose to the New Almaden mines, twelve miles away. Yes, indeed, quoth the up-and-a-coming Waters; if he could not do that very thing, where was the individual to be found that could? And as to the quality of the horses, were they not of pure Hambletonian blood? and would they not obliterate the space between San Jose and the New Almaden mines in about the time it would take the wind to go? Well, but, Mr. Waters, are you aware as to whom you are speaking on the subject of the quality of horse flesh?

It was squarely demanded of Waters if he had ever been in Wisconsin—and it was reasonably well intimated to him that if he had not been there, that his observation and acquaintance with the animal called the horse was to be considered as hardly complete. Furthermore, he was clearly informed that the party with whom he was treating could accept of no "plugs" to perform this journey to the New Almaden mines, and that smooth words and high-sounding pedigrees were not what was wanted as much as good, strong, powerful animals. Waters admitted that the talking part was about as good on one side as the other, and hitched on two animals of the kind demanded to a nice three-seated vehicle with ample room.

Our party went forth this bright morning armed and equipped with lunch baskets, filled with all-abounding and delicious food to be partaken of upon the mountains.

The road from San Jose to the Reduction Works of this great Quicksilver Mining Company at the foot of the Coast Range, is twelve miles in length, and is as smooth and hard as a house floor. The horses made good what their master had claimed for them, and paced off the road in good style. We were passing through magnificent wheat fields, some well up, others just coming up, and others being put in, while others were still being plowed. We passed splendid vineyards, large orchards of pears, apricots, almonds and small fruits.

This Santa Clara Valley is said to be one of the finest in the State. In its center sits the city of San Jose, with its twenty thousand inhabitants, with handsome houses and grounds, fine blocks of buildings, elegant school houses and other public buildings, distant fifty miles nearly south from San Francisco.

It took us about two hours to make the journey from the city to the Reduction Works of the New Almaden, which are at the foot of the mountain. But then, you see, while my friend Waters' horses could have brought us on the journey in less time, we had many stops to make, for we had not a few questions to ask as we rode along this beautiful road, and country, on that bright forenoon as to what was the value of land, of horses, cattle, etc.

The little village at the works, composed entirely of the people connected with them, is called Hacienda. As we enter it, we first come to the large mansion and handsome grounds of Mr. Randall, the Superintendent of the mine. The roadway is lined with shade trees, and a bright stream of water runs by the side of the road.

A polite and intelligent gentleman, long connected with the mines, showed us through the works, explaining the whole process of reducing the precious commodity from the ore. The ladies and the young people thought it a curious sensation to thrust their hands into the liquid metal as it stood in the kettles, preparatory to being put into the iron bottles or flasks, for shipment.

Having completed our observation of the process of reduction, we resumed our seats in the carriage and commenced the ascent of the mountain, where the mine is, and from whence comes the ore. The distance is two miles, and the elevation may be two thousand feet, perhaps more. Another village and church, called Almaden, is up the mountain. No visitors are admitted into the mine, which goes deep down into the bowels of the mountain, and we are content with a view of the handsome landscapes which stretch away before us, reaching far on towards the bay and city of San Francisco, commanding this beautiful valley.

But the time has come to find our picnic ground and partake of our repast. Here on this mountain side, where we spread our blankets and robes, it is as warm and pleasant as summer with us There is no water on this mountain height, and the inhabitants of Almaden have their water all brought up in casks upon the backs of donkeys. I went to the decent house of one of the citizens of Almaden, who was a Mexican, and asked for water, which he hospitably furnished, declining compensation.

What a royal feast was that, sharpened by our ride and the advancing afternoon, taken upon a grassy slope of the Almaden Mountain in the coast-range of the Pacific Ocean.

This quicksilver mine was discovered by the Spaniards so late as somewhere about 1840. The discoverers sold it to an English company, who developed it and made much from it, and in turn sold it to a New York company now carrying on the mine. Its production last year amounted to about 20,000 flasks. Each flask contains about seventy pounds. The price of the article is, say forty cents per pound, making the value of each flask $25 or more, and the whole production of the mine for the year to reach the sum of $500,000.

The Gaudeloupe mine, in the immediate neighborhood of the New Almaden, produces three-fourths as much, or 15,000 flasks.

The California quicksilver mines produced last year 73,000 flasks, while Spain produced but 40,000, and Austria but 10,000; so that it would appear that the quicksilver mines of California surpass those of Europe, and, for ought I know, of Asia besides.

Four happy brilliant days marked our stay at the bright city of San Jose, in the charming valley of Santa Clara. Our stay was made the more agreeable from the generous hospitality extended to us by our old Fourth Ward neighbors, Mr. and Mrs. Walter J. Moody, who we were happy to find most pleasantly circumstanced in their new home. They introduced us to many cultivated and pleasant people, and showed us the many handsome places with which the city and its surroundings abound. We now go by railroad up the San Waukeen (San Joaquin) Valley to Los Angeles.   E. D. H.

LETTER X.

Los Angeles, the Beautiful City in the Valley of St. Gabriel—Its Fruit Farms, Vineyards, and Landscapes—Methods of Farming in Lower California.

LOS ANGELES, Cal., Feb. 16, 1880.

I last wrote you from the fertile and pleasant valley of Santa Clara and the bright, attractive city of San Jose (pronounced San Hosay). From thence we came here by rail, a distance of some 400 miles by the Central & Southern Pacific Railroad. The trend of this road is about southeast and nearly the same as that of the sea coast until the coast reaches Point Conception, off Santa Barbara, when it turns more eastward and the railroad a little westward, and the two come together within fifteen miles at this point.

The Southern Pacific Railroad proper leaves the old overland road at a point called Lathrop, in the valley of the San Joaquin, about equi-distant from Sacramento and San Francisco, and then pushes up this greatest of California's valleys, the San Joaquin (pronounced San Waukeen), for 250 or 300 miles. I was very sorry that we had to make this part of the journey, through this great wheat, cattle and sheep producing valley, in the night. But so it was. The morning light found us out of the valley, and revealed wide-spreading hills and mountains, and our route was winding along their sides, and doubling our former track, and in one instance actually going around the cone of a mountain, and *crossing* our track where we had just passed eighty feet below, being that piece of this road called "The Loup." For a hundred miles this road runs along the sides and over the crests of these mountains. They are bored by numerous tunnels.

Live oak and mountain pine abound. Little or no underbrush obtains, while grass, now green and bright, makes a handsome landscape, and abounding pasture for sheep and cattle, seen along the road. The cost of this piece of road, over and through these mountains, must have been very heavy, and drawn largely upon the surplus funds of the Central Pacific to have built it.

Nor does the enterprise and power of this corporation stop here. It has pushed on and is nearly at Tucson, in Arizona, six hundred miles from here, and within three hundred miles of El Paso, at the western corner of Texas, where it will be met by the Texas Pacific Road. Also, it is said, that the Atchison, Topeka & Santa Fe Road will soon be at Fort Craig, in the Valley of the Rio Grande, which is within three hundred miles of either Tucson or El Paso. So that, in the near future, it is certain that the Southern Pacific Railroad will be an accomplished fact, opening immediate and, it is to be hoped, prosperous communication with all the Southern and Southwestern parts of the country, and let that day be speeded on, and may the Crockers, Standfords and Huntingtons, and their associates, have much credit and prosperity for their bold enterprise in opening up this great highway over mountains and through deserts, that the two sides of the continent may have another iron band to cement and bind its interests in unity, and all this without any money subsidy from the Government. Withal, it is a well-built, well-appointed and well-managed road.

This city of Los Angeles is a bright handsome town of 15,000 inhabitants. You know what the meaning of the name is, don't you? Don't know. Well, I must tell you. "The place or home of the angels." Is not that a fine name? It rather makes the blood tingle in your veins—makes the light come in your eye, and your tongue to wag in poetic strains to think of it. Yea, more; it summons one up to be a purer and better person, this living and being at the home of the angels!

But what right or claim, you may well enquire, has this place to be called "the home of the angels?" Much the same right, no doubt, that has authorized the use of so many saints' names to be given to places, and towns, by the Spanish priests who came to this country and took possession of it one hundred years ago. If saints and angels take any interest in places that are named after them, and have any power over affairs in this " mundane sphere," California ought to be a wonderfully good place and country, for the number of towns, rivers, valleys and mountains named after saints is very great.

But has Los Angeles the right, allegorically or otherwise, to be called the home of the angels? I take some stock in the affirmative side of this question.

A range of mountains starts off abruptly from the ocean, and runs almost due east for a long distance, say fifty or sixty miles, when they curve away to the south and east. At the base of this range of mountains, flows out an undulating and beautiful country, abounding with flowing streams and springs. In the centre of this plain, and in the midst of gentle hills, beautiful for situation, did the angels make their home, and here is the city named after them.

I think I can quite well understand their argument, when they selected this spot. It is evident that Gabriel was among them, for one of the most beautiful of all the valleys is named after him— and in his argument for locating here I think I see him pointing his fellows to that range of mountains I have spoken of, and saying, "See how the north wind, and the west wind, with their snow and their cold from Alaska, must stand back and stay behind, while the sunlight from glorious morn to dewy eve, shall pour its rich effulgence forever into this Edenic spot." Thus spoke Gabriel and all the brethern said "Amen."

We came here on a Tuesday It rained that day, and we hastened to find a home that should be in accord with the name and spirit of the place. This we did at the hostelrie of Mr. Strowbridge, an unpretentious place called the "White House." Like all angelic things, it proved better than it promised. Settled, and rested, we are ready for work. We can do much on foot. The postoffice, the hotels, the principal streets, and public buildings, are sought out and viewed, and some eminence may be gained, but it may be well supposed that the home of beings with wings, able to make wide and swift circuits, has breadth and great circumference. Such, indeed, has Los Angeles; and, having no wings, we must look out for the best blooded California horses. Taking my young friend Baker, late from New Hampshire, for my guide, we visited numbers of livery stables. At one, the man was away; at another, the buggies were all out; at another, the buggies were, too, all out, but seeing this was the case the owner said, "I have a nice two-seated carriage and a span of horses which I think you will like and which I should like to have you drive."

I had already talked with this man, and found that he had worked as a tinner under Mr. Charnley on the Court House at Milwaukee. This circumstance brought us into new relations, and made matters run very smoothly, even angelic. The team he gave me—the harness, and the carriage, were all, to say the least, that human beings need to have.

It was noon before we got started. These horses far surpassed Water's horses at San Jose, which I wrote you were a good span of horses. It took all my strength to hold them. All the roads are splendid in this country. We took a wide sweep over hill and dale, amid orange groves and lemon groves, laden with fruit, almond groves, walnut groves and vineyards. The towering rose bushes, geraniums, heliotropes, and other plants, in blossom, made the air fragrant with their odors. The lawns, fields and hills were clothed in their tenderest green. The summits of the mountains in the distance were covered with snow. As the afternoon sunlight came streaming over these enchanting landscapes, coloring and bedecking them with exquisite tints, we cried out and said—" Yes, fit home for the angels!"

So full of interest was this ride that, Gibbs, the owner of the team, was requested on the next occasion for a ride to have his establishment on hand early in the morning. I had now studied my lesson, and found that I must make a long heavy day's ride to witness the best specimens of farming and horticulture that the region afforded. This was found in the Valley of San Gabriel. It particularly embraced the Indiana settlement, or Pescadero, and the extensive farms of Shorb, Titus, Rose & Baldwin, besides many other smaller places. The drive, with the outs and ins, would equal forty miles.

Mrs. Holton and Master Neddie James are on the back seat, young Baker and your humble servant are in front. For the want of a better driver, I assume the reins. They go, and that right along. Never before, and not since, when, with Gov. Smith we spent those wonderful eighteen days in Old Egypt, have I seen any such sunlight, transparency and luminousness of atmosphere as characterize the days here in Southern California. They are much alike.

The Indiana settlement is eight or ten miles northeast of Los Angeles. This settlement was started some seven years ago upon virgin land by Indiana people. It is situated directly before the Sierra Madre Mountains, upon an open, undulated plain. To-day it is a garden spot. Handsome dwellings rise up amid orange and lemon groves, and occupy a wide expanse of country. Admirably-made roads and churches and school-houses attest the character of the people. A system of water works, carried by iron pipes, spreads through this settlement, affording water for irrigating and other purposes. In the midst of this community has our late fellow-citizen, Mr. Markham, made his home. He has twenty-two acres, mostly planted in oranges; a handsome cottage house and surrounding conveniences; altogether a pleasant and desirable home. We made a pleasant call upon Mr. and Mrs. Markham, and were glad to find that Mr. M., who was obliged to leave Milwaukee on account of rheumatic troubles, had found here entire relief and health. Here, too, we met Mr. Shadbolt, from our city, who had come for health and was finding it.

From Pescadero we drove on to Sierra Madre Villa. This is directly at the foot of the range of mountains, of which I have spoken, and is a hotel for invalids and visitors, much frequented. In this locality are numerous bee ranches, where bees, gathering honey from the sage, and other blossoms on the mountains, accumulate large quantities of honey annually.

Turning eastward, we drive through some open and enclosed pastures—quite dense in some places with live oak and other timber, passing some fine wheat and barley fields. We come to Mr. Titus' ranch or farm. To this gentleman my old friend Mr. Geo. O. Tiffany had given me a note of introduction. Mr. Titus was at home and gave us a cordial welcome. He came from Hamburg, Erie County, N. Y., nine years ago, and bought a portion of what is his present farm of 230 acres. He is himself an able-bodied and hard-working man. And an overlook of his place and a prolonged conversation with him was most satisfactory. The following are some items given me by him, which will show something of farming in Southern California.

Mr. Titus has 3,650 orange trees in bearing, 1,500 lemon trees, 1,200 lime trees, besides apricots, peaches, pears, pomegranates, walnuts, olives, and apples, to the number of 250, and six and a half acres of grapes. He will realize from his oranges and lemons alone this year not less than $25,000 or $30,000. He took for his grapes, just as they came from the vines last year, something over $1,000. He raises corn, barley and wheat at pleasure. He has water in abundance for irrigating his entire farm. I suppose this farm would be valued as high as $80,000. I must not pass Mr. Titus without speaking of the hospitality extended to us by his two accomplished daughters, in their pleasant home.

From Mr. Titus' we drove to the extensive establishment of L. J. Rose, whom we found at home, and from whom we learned the following facts: He occupies 1,900 acres of land; upon this land are 7,000 orange trees, fifteen years old; 500 English walnut trees, reasonably remunerative; besides apples, lemons, olives, figs, etc., which don't pay, and 510 acres of grapes. He is the greatest vintner in this country, and perhaps anywhere. Last year he manufactured 220,000 gallons of wine and bought 90,000 gallons, and manufactured 47,000 gallons of brandy. Beside his own grapes, he bought the grapes from 106 other vineyards. Mr. Rose came from Keokuk, Iowa, nineteen years ago, and is an educated German. He has planned this establishment and brought it to its present high state of perfection by his own genius. I have never seen better husbandry than his place shows. He has at times been heavily in debt, but it is said that he now has the means of paying it off, while his income is steadily increasing.

From Rose's we drove on three miles to Baldwin's. This man, who is the owner of the Baldwin Hotel at San Francisco and one of the California millionaires, has in his ranch fifty-six thousand acres of land. We drive for miles through it. Baldwin has elegant houses, stables, fishponds, immense fields of oranges and other fruits, wheat fields, etc. But he is an *absentee* farmer. It was interesting to go through his extensive grounds, drives and parks, but his place lacks the culture which personal attention affords, as shown in the places of Titus and Rose.

My advice to Baldwin is to cut up his vast tract of land and sell it out to small farmers. The holding of these extensive bodies of land is an evil in any country, and a crying one in California.

We are fifteen miles from home. The heads of "Dundee" and "Sarah Ann" are turned thither, and they are bidden to go, and they go.

The Valley of San Gabriel is a fit appendage to the "home of the angels."

I need to say that I find our former worthy fellow citizens, Mr. and Mrs. Geo. O. Tiffany in good health and pleasantly situated.

E. D H.

LETTER XI.

Santa Barbara—Beautiful Scenery—Big Farms—Enormous Crops.

SANTA BARBARA, Cal., March 1, 1880.

In my last, written from Los Angeles, I explained to you the meaning of that name—that it was the "home of the angels," and gave my opinion that so far as I knew and could judge the angels made an excellent selection for their home. But since I have come up here to Santa Barbara I am not quite clear that they made the best choice. The people of Santa Barbara say, without a dissenting voice, that they did not, and I am half inclined to their opinion, and still I cannot quite settle down to it, because I dare not set up my opinion against so astute a judgment as that of Gabriel, who doubtless must have been of the number at Los Angeles. And I cannot doubt that with his facility and power of locomotion he must have looked over this place before settling at the other.

But be all that as it may, this undoubtedly is to be set down as a singularly charming spot. The conditions for securing a soft and delightful climate seem perfect. The sea from a point forty miles to the west of Santa Barbara turns in its trend and runs almost due east for a distance of fifty or sixty miles. A wall of mountains from 3,000 to 4,000 feet high follow this trend of the sea along the entire distance, standing back from the shore from three to six miles, leaving a bench of land diversified with hills and swelling lands of charming mould, on some of which grow some of the grandest evergreen oaks that human eye ever beheld.

It is in one of the choicest of spots on this elongated beach that Santa Barbara is located. Just behind the town on the north stands Monte Cita, stretching along two miles to the east from the old Mission. This is covered with freshest green; residences dotting it here and there on its side and top.

Immediately beyond rise the bald, rugged mountains, gashed and slitted, leaving their sharp peaks pointing high in the heavens. There is nothing on these mountains save some patches of chapparel and sage brush.

On the south stretches along just on the shore of the sea a grass and vineyard covered hill, very handsome in its moulding. This high land has a length of three miles.

An admirable elevation of plain land lies between these heights, of a mile and a half in width. At its east end the sea has turned north and pushed itself toward the mountains, making with the islands lying off in the distance an excellent and safe roadstead or harbor.

To the west this table of land runs out indefinitely. In this valley and on this plain is located the charming little city of Santa Barbara, with its handsome houses and unparalleled gardens—to-day all laden with roses and calla lilies, geraniums and every other species of gorgeous flower. It has large and commodious hotels, blocks of brick stores, spacious and handsome churches and school-houses, and a college. I do not know its population, but judge it to be, say, four or five thousand. There is a sprinkling of the old Mexican population and some Chinamen here, but the bulk of the people are Eastern, with many from New England. The Mayor of the town is the son of Joseph Chamberlain who, with his brother Selah, had so much to do with the early construction of railroads in Wisconsin—a fine gentleman.

A public library is maintained and a club of sixty gentlemen. Mr. Ford, an artist from Chicago, has a private picture gallery mostly of California landscapes which would be a credit to any public gallery.

It will be seen, then, that the topographical conditions are such as to make almost a perpetual summer at Santa Barbara. Do you ask if at the highest altitude of the sun the heat does not become insufferable? A negative is given to the question on account of the contiguity of the ocean, which daily tempers this heat in summer, and in like manner, combined with the action of the sun, prevents frost in winter.

For persons afflicted with weak lungs and any tendency to pulmonary diseases there are many places in Southern California that will give them delightful relief. This place, especially, will always be resorted to with great satisfaction, not only on account of its health-giving blessings, but for the beauty of its scenery and the high social, religious and intellectual character of its population.

Conspicuous among the many interesting persons it has been my pleasure to meet in California, is Col W. W. Hollister, of this place. Shall I tell you his story? He is now, say, fifty. He is a native of Ohio, a graduate of Kenyon College. He came to California among its early immigrants. He saw what could be done with sheep, and, leaving gold hunting and every other pursuit, he returned to Ohio, borrowed $7,000, bought a flock of 2,000 of the best blooded sheep he could find, and started with them for California. He reached Salt Lake City at the beginning of the first winter, and there wintered. In the spring he pushed on, taking a southerly route through Arizona, and entering Southern California, came to this place on his journey to some point as near San Francisco as he could get and find pasturage for his flock. When he arrived here, his flock had diminished from two thousand to eight hundred. At a point fifteen miles west by north from this place he came to a spot in this, then, wilderness, where he laid himself down with his flock to rest. It was near the sea. Behind him lay the Santa Inez Mountains. At their feet were gently moulded foot hills, covered with mighty evergreen oaks, presenting such a picture of beauty as the Queen of England never looked upon, while the rich plain land spread out for five miles to the ocean. Here this young man, who, with such courage and fortitude, had come three thousand miles over great rivers and fertile lands, populous with people and many handed industries—and over vast and almost interminable plain, desert and mountain-lands with scarce an inhabitant, arose from his rest and surveyed the scene around him and declared that it surpassed in all natural beauty anything his eyes had ever before beheld, and then and there made his vow that should he be prospered in his work and life he would here come and found his home.

Waking up his sheep and bidding them follow, he wended his way toward the great centre of California—viz., San Francisco, and in that vicinity (Monterey County) he settled. For two years he herded his sheep alone, staying with them by day and by night. For, as he told me, "I was too poor to hire anybody to help me." Now, settled in their abiding place, and rested, the flock throve and multiplied apace. In time a few hundred ewes were added— less than five hundred—and such was the attention given by the master to his flock, so well were they guarded and treated, that, while other's flocks were diseased and starved and died, his continued in good condition, and in a few years reached eighty thousand head.

Mr. Hollister confined himself strictly to his sheep business, and, as he puts it, each one of his first flock of eight hundred head earned him $1,000. His wealth grew apace—and nine years ago he came back to that spot which was so beautiful to his youthful poetic nature, and purchased of that land nearly four thousand acres, and has made of that spot an earthly paradise indeed.

It is named Glen Anna, the latter part of the name being that of his accomplished wife, who dispenses the hospitality of her beautiful home—as we had occasion to konw—in a charming manner. Upon this land Col. H. has planted within the nine years since he took it in a state of nature, the following fruit-bearing trees: 25,000 almond; 3,000 English walnut; 600 olive;

1,200 orange; 1,000 lemon; and 500 lime trees. Besides these, the number of cypress, pine, eucalyptus (an evergreen from Australia of great merit), and other ornamental and useful trees, is almost unlimited.

The day we were there the whole 25,000 almond trees were in full bloom. I should say that the blossom was much like the peach —somewhat whiter. It was a remarkable sight to look over this immense forest of blooming trees. He expects that his almond trees, which are just now coming into bearing, will produce for each tree at least one dollar's worth of almonds. As a farmer, he raises wheat, barley, corn, buckwheat, and potatoes. Wheat has gone as high as fifty-two bushels to the acre, and 1,800 bushels of sweet potatoes have been taken from one acre of land. Five crops of barley have been taken from one plowing, and some of the land will reproduce from its own seeding perpetually.

Besides crop farming, he keeps large flocks (or bands as they are called in this country) of sheep, cattle, horses and swine, and believes in, and practices, diversified farming.

Upon the place are two large centres, one called the Ranch House, where the foreman lives, and where are the large barns and out-buildings, and where the chief business of the place is conducted. The other place up the Glen and under the mountain, is the family home. At each of these centres are gardens in splendid cultivation, filled with all manner of beautiful flowers. This comes of having a cultivated woman at the head of these affairs, learned in all the lore of horticulture. From one of her beds of calla lillies in the open garden last Easter she cut fifteen hundred flowers, and their absence would hardly be noticed. Think of that, you ladies who wait so long and labor so patiently to secure a single flower, and when out, call in all your neighbors to behold the sight!

Col. Hollister is not only thus a great and enterprising farmer, but he has given a helping hand to all the principal improvements at Santa Barbara. Hotels, wharves, churches, schools and handsome blocks of buildings have all received a helping hand from his munificence. Besides, he has found time to promote and secure the passage of many laws in aid of agriculture, and written with much ability and at length upon the relations of capital and labor. He has honored himself and his State in these directions, and is deserving of much praise at the hands of his fellow citizens.

Here at Santa Barbara we had the pleasure of meeting our friend and neighbor Col. Yates and his son Arthur, and were inmates of the hospitable home of Dr. and Mrs. Phelps, all combining to make pleasant our stay at this delightful spot. Wherever else you go, or do not go, fail not when you come to California to visit Santa Barbara. E D. H.

LETTER XII.

Back to San Francisco, Through the San Joaquin Valley—The Homes of California Millionaires—Enormous Farms.

SAN FRANCISCO, Cal., March 15, 1880.

My last letter was sent you from Santa Barbara—the land of sun and beauty. From that place we made our way by eighty miles of good honest staging, conducted along this coast by a stage company of which, if I mistake not, Major Warren, of Albany, in our State, is a member. From Santa Barbara to Buena Ventura, a distance of thirty miles, the journey was made upon the beach of the sea with the waves rolling betimes well up upon the horses' legs and the wheels of the coach. My little grandson, Neddie, seeing the waves coming in so stoutly upon us, was wont to cling to his grandmother and otherwise give expression to his fears.

I rode with the driver and he would now turn away from the hard sand, washed by the waves, into the soft sand some feet higher, just under the foot of the mountain—for the mountain crowded the road close to the sea much of the way. When I asked him why he turned thus, he replied, that just beyond where he did so, lay quick sand that would swamp us if we approached it. Indeed! and is your path so treacherous as that? Yes. But the other day a traveler got in there and came near destruction. Well, then, let us keep well away from quick sands of all kinds, physical and moral, for they are terrible indeed!

At Ventura we leave the sea and drive northeast fifty miles up the narrow valley of the Santa Clara River to Newhall, where the Southern Pacific Railroad is reached.

The last twenty-five miles of this ride took us through the wheat fields of one man, H. M. Newhall, of this city. His ranch embraces forty-nine thousand acres, much of it to be sure in mountain land, but along the stream is much fine meadow—and upon these meadows stretching along this twenty-five miles he has now in wheat ten thousand acres, which is looking very well, as abundant rain has fallen in this region. At the station Mr. Newhall has built a fine public house in which are a store and offices conducted by Mr. Field, his foreman and partner, a cultivated and practical youngerly man from Massachusetts. Mr. Field gave me a splendid ride through the wheat fields and pleasant forests around. All was system, order and excellence under his administration. The hotel here is warmed by open fire places, and Mr. Newhall (who is a Massachusetts man), has shown his Yankee pedigree by building a fireplace after the style of his great grandfather, six feet wide, four feet high, and three feet deep. This is located in the great sitting room into which the stage passengers arrive and from which they depart. In this fire place, as we came, was an immense back log glowing with a red heat, with a great bed of coals in front, and was it not a glory indeed after a long ride in the cold night air to come before it?

Besides this ranch, Mr. Newhall owns two others of equal size, making him the owner of one hundred and fifty thousand acres of land. I had the pleasure of making this gentleman's acquaintance in this city. He has long conducted the auctioneer's business, and is reputed to be very wealthy. Indeed, he told me that by a favorable turn in some of his business affairs a few years since he had so much money that he did not know what to do with it, and as he did not want stocks, purchased these lands. I enquired if they had proved profitable. No—they had not.

One of the great evils of California is the holding of these vast bodies of land by a few people.

I venture to suggest to Mr. Newhall that in the presence of so much disturbance of the labor question, and in the presence of so many homeless people, he could do no better thing for himself and for them, than to cut up these lands, so far as he might be able to do so, and sell them to actual settlers. The truth is that the larger proportion of the area of California is mountainous and may not be reduced to arable land. But there remains much that could be added to the present farming land of the State, and it would be far better for the interest of all concerned, if such owners as Mr. Newhall would parcel out their lands and sell them to actual owners and occupants.

From Newhall we pass over the dreadful Mojave Desert for fifty or sixty miles, and as much more of broken mountain country, and drop into the upper end of the Waukeen Valley (San Joaquin) and have a splendid drive down through its wide-spreading wheat fields to where it joins the waters of the bay. We had to pass through this widest and best valley in California, when we went south, in the night, and thus lost a sight of it. But now we came upon it in the early morning, and it was radiant with beauty along its entire length. Wheat, wheat, wheat, upon either hand as far as the eye could reach, and all looking in fine condition. A common complaint made of this San Joaquin Valley is that, as a rule, it is too dry, and there is not sufficient water to irrigate it except in limited portions. To-day the promise is good for fine crops this season throughout its wide extent.

It is along the west side of San Francisco Bay that a number of the millionaires of the city have gone to make their summer homes. It is a handsome bench of land lying between the water and the coast range of mountains or high hills, with groves of evergreen oaks of much splendor at certain spots. Ralston was the first to lead off in establishing these splendid places, and built "Belmont," twenty-five miles away from the city. Here in his time he dispensed a princely hospitality, and any stranger visiting California, bringing fair letters of introduction, was taken to his home, without money, and without price, in magnificent turnouts, and entertained in the most courtly and generous manner.

D. O. Mills followed, and built an elegant place seventeen miles from the city. But at Menlo Park, thirty-three miles down, a trio of these millionaires have tried to see what they could do. Nature, by hill and dale, and sweet meadow land, tried her hand at beauty, and succeeded well. Then followed Senator Latham, and built one of the most tasteful mansions and surrounded it with such beautiful ornamentation that it may challenge anything at home or abroad to surpass it. It is said that one and a quarter millions of dollars went into the place. But oh, the vanity of riches. Latham is a bankrupt and has left this home and the State. He is a cultured and high class man.

Next follows Stanford, the President of the Central Pacific, and a former resident of Port Washington. He has a farm of some thousands of acres, and maintains a stud of three hundred horses, some of them valued at many thousands of dollars. His house is not much, but his grounds, his drives, his fences and outbuildings are on a grand scale and are in fine order. He is spoken of by his neighbors as a worthy citizen.

Next follows Flood, of Bonanza fame. His grounds are equally extensive and are covered with many fine trees. But the land is flat and monotonous. He is just now having a house built which is of immense proportions, and I should say that he had given carte blanche to all the architects in the country to see how many peaks, and points, and pinnacles, and crinkles they could get on to it. I would call it a shoddy affair,—the whole arrangement a show of money, unaccompanied with taste or true art. Besides these splendid places, there are many minor ones along this road, combining beauty and good taste, and, though lesser in show and size, are doubtless happier homes.

Speaking of the millionaires of California, their number, so far as I can learn, is not large. They are made up of about five of the mining fraternity and about the same number of the Pacific Railroad men. Of the former stand in the list Flood, O'Brien, Mackay, Fair, and perhaps one other. Of this list O'Brien is dead. His estate was inventoried to be worth about $10,000,000.

These men are all Irishmen from the common walks of their countrymen. Among the railroad millionaires are Stanford, Huntington, Crocker, Hopkins, and one or two others whose names I do not recall. The average wealth of all these men is put at $10,000,000 each, and upwards, by the speech of people.

Of the Flood, O'Brien, Mackay and Fair ring much complaint is made of the conduct of affairs as managers of the Comstock Consolidated Mines, and suits are commenced against them for the recovery of money belonging to stockholders, and on this account the O'Brien estate is not distributed. These men show their wealth in sumptuous living, and are not known as doing anything in the way of public benefaction.

The railroad men above named were originally a set of plain merchants doing business at Sacramento, who were the first to comprehend and to take hold of the Pacific Railroad on this end, and to boldly step forth to promote its accomplishment. Their courage, sagacity and perseverance is worthy of all admiration. Not only did this set of men build this end of the Pacific road for 800 miles, but they have run excellent railroads over the most of the State, and all these roads are first-class and conducted in the very best manner. There is a good deal of scolding about the monopolistic character of this great corporation, and probably not without reason. At the same time it must be set down as a great benefaction to the State.

These men in turn make a good deal of show of their money in the way of fine house building. Hopkins, particularly, who is credited as having been the clearest headed of them all, and who all his life had lived in almost narrow circumstances, observing the sharpest economy, finally erected an immense palace, some say at a cost of $1,500,000, on the apex of one of the highest hills overlooking San Francisco. The outlook from it is truly magnificent. But hardly had this enterprising man completed his castle before he was called to close accounts with earth. A widow without children occupies the place, and the house stands rather a monument of the man's folly than otherwise.

I cannot learn that any of these men have done, or intend to do, any philanthropic act for the promotion of any great public interest. How much better if, instead of putting a million and a half of dollars into a dwelling that is not worth ten cents on a dollar, and is only a by-word in the mouths of sensible men, Mr. Hopkins, like Amos Lawrence, and Mr. Vassar, and Mr. Cornell, and Judge Packard, had put it into some institution of learning and science, that, like a river, would have run on forever to bless the people of this interesting State, where he had gained his own great pecuniary prosperity! When will rich men learn what are the higher and better uses of money? It is this selfish and baser use of wealth that gives, in part, to the Denis Kearneys food for agitation.   E. D. H.

LETTER XIII.

The Great Sonoma Valley — Petrified Forests — The Geysers — The People Who Live in the Beautiful Valley.

SACRAMENTO, March 25, 1880.

The Geysers are located in the Sonoma range of mountains, about one hundred miles due north from San Francisco. Two routes lead to them; one up the west side of the range, along the Sonoma valley, and the other up the east side by the Napa Valley. A railroad goes up each of these valleys. From the end of the road leading up the Sonoma Valley, the staging into the mountains is sixteen miles to this natural phenomenon, while from the eastern or Napa side it is just twice that distance. It is on this latter route that Foss lives, the most celebrated "whip" perhaps in the country, and still conducts passengers from Calistoga at the end of the railroad along this thirty two miles of mountain pass to the Geysers. He, himself, now no longer drives. A few years since he was driving his six in hand with some young fiery horses in his team dashing along the mountain road, when one of his reins gave away, and his team became unmanageable and dashed his coach in pieces and killed a lady passenger, since which time, as the story goes, he has not driven, but has surrendered this office to his son.

Kennedy is the owner of the stage line from Cloverdale at the terminus of the Sonoma Valley Railroad, and drives his own teams. In the season of travel these two stage lines and the railroads make regular running connections, so that the traveler may make the circuit ever so nicely, going up the one valley and coming down the other. But now there are no running arrangements established for going into the mountains. It is too early, and doubtful if the roads are open. But, receiving the assurances from Mr. Hughes, General Manager of the Sonoma Valley Road (San Francisco & Northern Pacific), that the way was certainly open from the end of his road, and the distance by stage but sixteen miles, this route was adopted.

It was 3 o'clock in the afternoon when we bade adieu to San Francisco. We had said good bye to our many pleasant acquaintances made in that wonderful city. . The day was bright as are all the days of this sunny country—yes indeed! How sunny. In the seventy days we have been in California there have been but eight rainy and cloudy days, and this they call the rainy season. From this time on they expect but little or no rain until November. The possibilities of production from the land particularly by reason of the continued fine weather, are very great, and yet I think, upon the whole, the present population make but poor use of these advantages.

In making this journey to the Geysers by the Sonoma route, thirty-six miles of it is made by steamer along the northern prong of the glorious San Francisco Bay. We step on to the Donahue steamer near the foot of Market street, and away we go. The afternoon is still and calm; the water is smooth as glass. We pass great ships lying at anchor waiting for wheat cargoes to Liverpool. This Bay of San Francisco could easily harbor in safety all the ships in the world. At our right lies Vallejo, up another prong of the bay into which comes the Napa river. At this place the Government has a naval station employing a large force of men, and to which point rendezvous all the ships of the Government for repair and outfit, I suppose, on this coast.

On our left is San Quentin, where stands out conspicuously the State's prison with its thousand inmates, and I have heard it said composed mostly of young men—sad thonght! God speed the day when virtue shall stand in the place of vice. Young man, go to your Maker and ask Him for help, that you may withstand the power of the wicked One.

Further on upon our left is San Rafeal, with its three thousand inhabitants, sweetly nestled in a cove under the high green hills. Its white houses and edifices looked in the distance like a flock of doves cuddling in some cozy nook. We speed our way. The Bay narrows, it is now but a mile wide. On either side the hills shine in the afternoon sun in their gorgeous garments of emerald. Great flocks of ducks cover the water, and they are so tame that the steamer comes close upon them ere they deem it expedient to rise. Gulls in large numbers wheel and circle and call perpetually upon the scullion to throw over his offal, that they can have their supper, and when he does so, what a darting down and what a scuffle they have in the water for the precious morsels.

We are now in a river, and then run for a mile or two circling along through the marshy meadows, till we reach Donahue, a small village pleasantly situated, where we meet the railroad, and are off for a sixty or seventy mile ride up the Sonoma Valley to Cloverdale. We pass Petaluma with its six or seven thousand inhabitants. Fifteen miles beyond, Santa Rosa, of equal size. The valley is beautiful, and every where under fine cultivation. But now the night shuts down and we reach Cloverdale, and sleep at Herr Dutchman's. (I have forgotten his name.) He keeps quite a good hotel. He is well-acquainted with Milwaukee lager, and knows how to charge his guests for his accommodations a full price.

Bright and early Kennedy is on hand with his strong, good horses and coach for the Geysers. He gets into my confidence at once—not only on account of his handsome and manly bearing, but he is a native of New Hampshire, my native State; and, if you ever noticed it, the New Hampshire people, as a rule, are a decent set. Do you know if this is really true what has been said of the Switzer, that, taken away from his native Alps, and set down in a plain country, he dies of homesickness? There is something very fascinating about mountain scenery. They who live among it are doubtless hardier and stronger physically and mentally—other things being equal—than they who live in the plain land. Did you ever count up and see whether more and better poets did not come from the mountain than from the plain? Try it, and let us know. I am under the impression that the mountains make the poets.

Well, we start. We are the only passengers Kennedy has, and are the very first visitors to the Geysers in 1880. Leaving the pretty village of Cloverdale we drive for a little while by cultivated farms, on the Russian River, and soon enter the Pluton Canon, in the bottom of which flows one of the clearest and fullest brooks or small rivers I have seen in California. This stream would do honor to New Hampshire. It bounds, it dashes, it foams, it flashes, now gently, now noisily.

The mountain ribs and spurs shoot sharply down to the little river, pushing it now this way and now that. The road has been built at much expense. Now it hangs along the precipice high above the dashing stream. It is very narrow. Be careful, Kennedy, if we go off here it is all day with us. And thus we wind in and out along the crags and into dark ravines. The snows and rains of winter make sad havoc with these mountain roads. Slides of earth and stone come down from above and carry away whole sections. Many of these spots had just been repaired, and I was quite jealous of their solidity lest the weight of our horses and coach might start the new-made earth, yet saturated with wet, down, down, down into the yawning gulf.

But no. Kennedy said it was all secured, and so it proved, and at the end of three hours' steady pulling up the mountain we came safely to the comfortable hotel of the Geysers, and were cordially welcomed by Koch, the old guide, and by Mrs. Sherwood, the charming little housekeeper.

Business is business. It is 11 o'clock. The inmates of the hotel are expecting Foss up from the other side. If he should come, we would dismiss Kennedy, stay all night, and go with Foss to Calistoga and down the Napa Valley. But then his coming is uncertain, and we must do the Geysers before dinner and return with Kennedy to Cloverdale, provided, in the meantime Foss does not make his appearance.

Between our hotel and the mountain which forms what are called the Geysers, runs the dashing Pluton. The mountain from which the stream is descending is directly before us. We start upon our journey. It is very hot. I take off my coat and go in my shirt sleeves, taking the advice of Koch, the guide, so to do. Mrs. Holton and the little grandson are equipped as lightly as possible. We descend deep from the hotel and cross the Pluton, and at once commence the ascent of the mountain in a narrow canon amid sulphurous odors and sissing boiling steam.

For my own part I had not a very distinct idea as to what constituted this California wonder. In the old geographies the Iceland Geysers were laid down as great streams of hot water sent high in air. But here only steam is sent forth. We climb up the steep ascent and everywhere the earth is hot and the steam is issuing, and at certain points are springs of boiling water. The odor of infernal fumes of sulphur and brimstone has given much just license to name these sundry spots after his majesty the devil, as for example—the "devil's teakettle," where is a boiling pool of water giving off a terrible odor. And then there is the "devil's bake oven"—and his "medicine chest," where is found Epsom salts and other medicines, and his "paint shop," where are pigments of various colors, and so on, which the worthy Mr. Koch, the guide, called off, and we paused a moment to look at, when we tugged away up the canon of the mountain amid the steam and the fumes, and the terrible heat and noisy thundering below. At the end of three-fourths of a mile we come to the boundary of the territory comprising the Geysers, when happily we reach a resting place, which was much needed. Perspiration was bursting from every pore, and a weariness rarely experienced took hold of us. After resting for a little while we descended by another route, avoiding the hideous one through which we came and were soon back to our hotel.

After an hour's visit, Mrs. Shelden spread the daintiest dinner that, that, that— Well, I cannot say how good a dinner you ever ate, but this was most capital—venison steak of the first water, ham and eggs, pitchers of luscious cream, raised biscuit, excellent bread, vegetables of various kinds, apricot preserves, and mince pie "as was mince pie." Long life to you, Mistress Shelden, who have such a rare knack of making your guests comfortable and happy, and may many travelers come to the romantic spot where stands your hospitable house, and find the solace, the comfort and the happiness it is calculated to impart.

The dinner is over. The bill is paid. A hearty farewell is given to Koch, the guide, a man of years and wide experience in the world, and to good-looking, cheery and most capable Mistress Sherwood, and we step into friend Kennedy's stage coach, and descend the mountain at a rapid pace, and as the shadows of the evening come on we are again at Cloverdale, and under the roof of our worthy German landlord, of the United States Hotel, well prepared for the slumbers of the night. But now we have not seen the petrified forest, another California wonder, which lies on the east side of the Sonoma Ridge, and near to Foss' beat. This wonder, of course, must be visited, or a visit to California would be a failure, especially in the estimation of those who run the Petrified Forest business.

Therefore, we hop onto the railroad on which we came up, and run back to San Francisco, and hop onto the railroad that runs up the Napa Valley and stay at Napa City the same night.

If you ask every man in the valley of the Napa how it compares in quality with that of any other valley in California, without a dissenting voice they will declare it far superior. That it is a valley of fine land and fine cultivation is not to be denied. Large amounts of grapes are raised here. These grapes chiefly go into wine; some go into raisins. The raising of the raisin grape is to become a great industry in California. The lands here are valued at from $50 to $100 per acre. Napa is a pleasant little city of 5,000 inhabitants, deriving its business from the farming country around it. I had time before leaving in the morning to look into the public school, which I found to be excellent, testifying at once to the worth of the population of the bright shiny city of Napa.

At 10:30 A. M. the train comes on bound for Calistoga. We are aboard and fly along through wide wheat fields, vineyards, plum, cherry, peach, pear, apricot and almond orchards. Many handsome residences adorn the landscape during this beautiful morning ride.

It is high noon as we come to the termination of the road,—the small village of Calistoga. The valley has narrowed and the foot hills now close in upon the north, and say, "Stop, Mr. Railroad; if you go much further, you must butt your head against our rocky sides."

It is from here that Foss starts on his thirty-two miles mountain drive to the Geysers. The Petrified Forest lies about five miles from this point to the westward, in this same range of mountains in which are the Geysers, but not on the same road. Major Johnson, keeper of the Calistoga Hot Springs Hotel, an "up and a coming" man for the place, furnishes us with a span of lithe bay horses and top buggy for the drive to the "Petrified Forest." It is a good rig. California rigs are generally so. With the woman on my left and the boy between, we turn out of the village and are soon ascending the mountain along a good road. The new leaves are just peeping out. Many flowers bow and smile and say Welcome, along the road. By winding ways, now in sunlight, now in deep shade, we make our journey to the home of Charles Evans, the owner and custodian of the forest. His modest white Swedish house stands on an eminence in an enclosure with a picket fence of an acre of land. Behind his house is another small house, the receptacle of his collection of mountain curiosities.

At the entrance a sign notifies us that we have reached our destination, and gives the name of the person with whom we have to do. As we wheeled into the premises no living thing was in sight, and we lifted our voice, saying, "Evans, ahoy." Well, our use of the sailor's term was not so far out of the way. For this turned out to be Evans' history. A Swede, now sixty-four years old, a bachelor, hale and hearty, of fine size and make, as gentle and sweet in his nature as a woman. After sailing all his life in every sea he landed on this coast and took to the mountains to find him a homestead upon Government land, where he could build his cot and lay himself down to die in composure when the time should come for that event. Here he took 320 acres and in clearing up his land he came upon this geological wonder. It consists of several hundred trees turned to stone, covering perhaps one hundred acres of mountain land, and all lying with the tops to the south, and the roots to the north. These stone trees are mostly buried in the earth. Evans has uncovered several,—enough for specimens. The largest and best specimen of them which he has exhumed is one seventy feet long with a girth of thirty feet. There is but little taper in this length,—showing that in its glory as a tree it must have been of immense height. All the features of the tree remain. The bark is perfect, the knots there. Bruises and scars appear, and even charred places where fire had burned the tree are distinct and perfect.

It is an extraordinary and most impressive sight. When and how did the Almighty work this wonder? Let the scientists tell if they can.

We turned and walked down the pleasant path with the gentle Swede who lives alone. But he told us he had sent to Sweden for his sister to come and live with him. Last year he had two thousand visitors. The price of admission is fifty cents each. Thus his three hundred and fifty acres of Government land is turning to good account. E. D. H.

LETTER XIV.

Up the Sacramento River—The Town of Chico—Gen. Bidwell's Model Farm.

SACRAMENTO, March 25, 1880.

Having gone up and down the Sonoma Valley and up and down the Napa Valley, it remained, in order to obtain a completed view of Northern California, to make the tour of the valley of the Sacramento River as far as Reading, being the most northern point to which a railroad extends on the way to Oregon, a distance of 170 miles from here. With slight exceptions, all the railroads in California are owned and operated by the Central Pacific Company or by the same parties who own that road. I will here take the opportunity to say, having been over the main road and several of its branches, that, in my jugdment, the management is to be classed among the very best. The road bed is solid and smooth. Engines large and of superior workmanship and in thorough condition. Cars built for durability and service, and well appointed for the comfort of travelers. Particularly has the Central inaugurated a car with an admirable sleeping contrivance for the comfort of its *emigrant* passengers; so, that this class, traveling at about half price, càn go in as much comfort as the first-class passengers. The ferry accommodations for crossing the bay from Oakland to San Francisco are unsurpassed for elegance, magnitude, strength and dispatch, by anything in the country.

At Sacramento is one of the most splendid depots and eating houses on the continent. Cars, engines, depots, work-shops, offices and eating-houses are all kept scrupulously neat and clean.

No noise or confusion in any direction is heard. Every officer, from Mr. Towne, the Superintendent, down to the brakeman upon the train, is polite, reserved, noiseless and strictly devoted to his work.

Whatever may have been the overgifts or the undergifts of the people through the appropriations of Congress to the Pacific Road, or whatever may have been the vices or the virtues of the "Credit Mobelier"—certain it is, that a splendid highway has been made across the deserts and through the mountains, and that the same is conducted in the interest of safety and comfort to the great traveling public.

Before speaking of our trip up the broad valley of the Sacramento River I must say something of the city of Sacramento, the capitol of the State. It stands here upon the banks of the river, on a low, flat piece of ground. All the surrounding country is low, and it has often been overflowed by the high water of the river. In modern times they have filled some of the streets to a point above high water, and the railroad company in co-operation with the city authorities, have made an embankment for their own protection along the shore of the river, which affords substantial protection against the overflow of the city. The population of the city is put at 25,000, some say more. The sidewalks are made of plank, and a few of the main streets are paved with cobble stones. There are some pretty good buildings of brick and many low, poor buildings. There are many pretty residences, and some quite sumptuous. Stanford keeps a fine house here and so do the Crockers. Judge Crocker, attorney of the Central Pacific and one of the smaller stockholders, now deceased, not only built a fine house, but also a picture gallery of nearly equal size, and filled it with an elegant collection of rare paintings and opened it to the public.

The State House as seen from the front, is a singularly handsome structure of the Corinthian order of architecture. But seen from the side, it does not look so well. The dome, which is superb, is not placed in the centre of the edifice, but nearer the front than the rear, and accordingly the symmetry of the building is impaired when seen from any other point than the front. In the Bibliotheke of the Vatican at Rome the visitor will see Michael Angelo's original draft of St. Peter's, and will observe that the dome is placed in the centre of the edifice, the form of the building being that of a Greek cross. The services of Raphael being called in, he extended the choir into the form of the Latin cross, and this meeting the pontifical approval, the building was so constructed, leaving the dome to stand in the centre of the transcepts, hence the wonderful dome of that august building cuts but a poor figure as it is approached from the front. It appears therefore that architects, great and small, come short of perfection.

When I first approached the State House of California from the front, I called it about the handsomest building I had ever seen. But seen from its other sides, its claim for that opinion has to be discounted to some extent. Still it is an elegant edifice, and well suited for the purpose for which it is designed. Its cost was $2,200,000.

Gen. John Mansfield, long a citizen of Kenosha, in our State, is the Lieutenant Governor of California, and presides with much dignity and to great acceptance over the Senate. He extended cordial attentions during my several visits to the State House. Here I found that ancient warhorse of reform, Warren Chase, so long conspicuous in the early days of Wisconsin politics. He is a Senator. Mr. Chase introduced me to Gov. Perkins; also to a brother Senator of the name of Watkins, who was also a Wisconsin man, being from Troy, Walworth Co., so that our State is pretty well represented in the California Senate. Warren Chase is 67 years old, and is looking strong and well. He sends his warmest regards to our worthy fellow-citizen, Hon. C. Latham Sholes.

The Governor of California (Perkins) is a fine looking man of 40 years. He is from Maine, and began life as a merchant and miner in the northern part of the State, and removing to San Francisco became a shipping merchant of the firm of Goodall, Perkins & Co., maintaining a line of steamers to Oregon and to Southern California.

Gov. Perkins is spoken of in high terms. The members of the two houses appear to good advantage from casual observations. They are coping with some grave questions under the new Constitution, and make slow progress. Their work promises to be conservative and useful.

In conferring about my journey up the valley of the Sacramento with Lieut. Mansfield he recommended me very particularly to get off at Chico and view the beauty of that place and its surroundings, and to make the acquaintance of Gen. John Bidwell, one of the prominent men of the State and a very large farmer of that locality. We came to Chico as the night set in, and found excellent quarters in the spacious Chico Hotel. Upon coming to our apartment I sat me down and succumbed to a feeling of sadness. Had my better half been cross and cold and indifferent? for women will sometimes do just this thing, and it is a great source and just cause of sadness. No, not this. Had I got out of money in a far distant land, with nobody at hand to supply that most essential article in travel? No, not quite. What then? Why that old sprain of my left ankle had come back to worry and vex me. It had for some days been scolding and complaining that I had been tramp, tramp, tramping until it was out of all manner of patience and would stand it no longer, and I had been obliged that day to go and find a crutch and put it to use. And now at the end of a long and wearisome day as I mused that some of the most important part of the California journey was yet to be done, particularly the Yosemite business, and it might have to be done amid deep snows, the sadness came to think, that under such circumstances my good left foot had gone back on me.

In the morning I enclosed the card of introduction in a note to General Bidwell, in which I intimated that I was not swift of foot, and that, should he be in the neighborhood of the hotel, I wished he would come and see me. A messenger took it to his home. As I sat alone writing in the ladies' parlor of the hotel who should enter but a charmingly dressed lady, bright as the morning sun, and cheery as the meadow lark's mating song, demanding if I was

Mr. Holton. I was only too happy in such a presence to admit that I was. Whereupon she announced herself to be Mrs. Gen. Bidwell, and that she had come upon the commands of her husband, who was obliged to join a party of surveyors for the morning, and take possession of me and mine for the day. We must drive with her during the morning and the General would join us at dinner by 3 P. M., who would then visit and drive with us the balance of the day.

How sweet is generous, unselfish hospitality! We were the merest strangers to these folks. The most I had expected from Gen. Mansfield's pencil card of introduction was an exchange of a half hour's conversation with Gen. Bidwell upon subjects of common interest, perhaps giving some specialty to agriculture, of which he is a leading practitioner. In an hour Mrs. Bidwell came with her elegant carriage and horses and for three hours drove us through groves of spreading oaks along the banks of the clear flowing Chico Creek, by which the native grape vines hung in vast masses as they climb high upon the oaks, making great wide curtains, entirely shutting out the sun. And now we are passing the cherry orchard, where grow thousands of great trees producing in their season the most luscious fruit of all its varieties; and now the peach orchard, and now the pears, the apricots and other fruits. Passing from fields where the wide-spreading orchards are enclosed we enter the enclosure where are kept the diary animals, and now where are kept the fattening animals, and now where the sheep are herded, and now where are the horses. These fields each embrace hundreds of acres, for the farm has twenty-two thousand acres of as handsome land as lies under the sun.

Passing from the above-enumerated enclosures, we enter the great wheat fields, lying in bodies of from five hundred to a thousand acres each. Finely graded roads lead through these ramifying grounds, for the owner is a man of scientific precision. All of these roads are laid out with two ideas in view—those of utility and beauty. The road is now curved that it may pass under the arching branch of the wide, spreading oak—for some of these oaks span a breadth of sixty feet; and now it winds by the bank of the brook, that the song of its babbling waters may add to the charm of the scene; and now it strikes for a mile or more upon a dead line across or between the sweeping fields. Gen. Bidwell would be a marked man in any community. He is a large, well-made man of sixty years of age, and admirably preserved. He is a native of Pennsylvania, and came to California with Fremont as early as 1841, and is thus well versed in California affairs under Mexican rule. Indeed, his narration of facts of that period, embracing the minutest history of Capt. Sutter, and the advent of the Federal Government and the discovery of gold, was like the letting out of water, and I charged him that he "write a book." He served a term in Congress soon after the close of the war, and should have been made the Governor of the State, as he was clearly the choice of the people. But he is a man that will descend to none of the tricks of the politicians, and because he would not, the tricksters of the party beat him in the convention and beat themselves before the people.

If one man is to be the possessor of so large a body of land as that owned by this gentleman, it is refreshing to find him not only a good manager of his affairs, but to find him a man of broad public spirit and generous co-operation in all good measures. His laying out of the little city of Chico, now containing five thousand inhabitants, shows his good taste, and philanthropic character, in providing schools, churches and a public hall of large dimensions. In religious profession, Gen. and Mrs. B. are Presbyterian, and they are not afraid or ashamed to be known as such, and to carry their profession into practical life.

Beside his own elegant home, seventeen tenement houses, large barns and outbuildings, warehouses, a fine grist mill, capable of turning out one hundred barrels of flour per day, dot his extensive grounds. Everything about his premises is in the most perfect order. Gates, fences, roads and buildings, as well as fields, command your admiration.

But enough. The refinement and elegance of the inside of the house was in proportion to the beauty and grandeur of the outside. What concerns your humble servant most is how he will ever be able to requite such courtesies as he has received at the hands of these and other kindred souls in California.

We stopped at Marysville and drove by carriage into the mountains to visit the hydraulic gold mining still carried on in that locality. But time forbids an attempt to give any detail of that feature of California industry and production. ·E. D. H.

LETTER XV.

The Great Yosemite Valley—Mariposa—Fremont—Mountains and Waterfalls.

SACRAMENTO, March 27, 1880.

Neither at San Francisco or at Sacramento could I learn anything definite about getting into the Yosemite Valley. "The road is not open," was the common answer, "and the snows have been so deep that we can give no certain information as to when it is likely that the trip can be made."

Three wagon roads now lead into the Yosemite Valley, each departing from the line of the Southern Pacific Railroad. Two of these roads leave the railroad at Merced, 152 miles from San Francisco, the one leading on a more northerly route, via Coulterville, and reaching the Yosemite in a distance of something a little less than a hundred miles. The other, taking a lower and more southerly route, and passing Mariposa, reaches the valley in a distance of ninety miles. The third route, and that to which the railroad influence is given, and to which the most formidable of the stage companies is committed, and over which the most passengers will be likely to go, leaves the railroad at Madera, thirty-three miles beyond Merced, and going by Fresno Flats, the Big Tree Station, and Clark's, reaches the valley with ninety miles of stage riding.

One of the chief advantages of this route is that it passes the forest of big trees, and thus two birds are killed with the one stone. But this road goes along upon mountain heights and, at this writing, there is so much snow that it cannot be passed.

The time had come when, if we visited this wondrous exhibition of the Divine Hand in His work of creation, we must go, if ever.

A gentleman in San Francisco, having mining interests on the route and well versed in the country, had informed me that if I left the middle road at Mariposa and drove by carriage to Hite's Cove, a distance of twenty miles, I would then find an open trail that would, with twenty-two miles of horseback riding, take us to the valley.

This, then, I found to be the only route by which at this season of the year the journey could be made, if made at all. Therefore we made our way to Merced, for at this point the journey must be arranged for with a special outfit. Beside, my informant could not be certain that heavy snows had not come in, and that mountain slides had not occurred to suspend passage on this route.

Upon inquiry at Merced, I was informed that John McLenathan, an old livery keeper and stage man, was the best informed person upon the subject, and best qualified to conduct the expedition. To John McLenathan came I, and found him a man of fifty years of age—his hair white as snow, having upon him the marks of sobriety, good sense and capacity. In other words, one from whose general appearance you could "tie to," and in this manner our converse began:

"Mr. McLenathan, have you ever been to the Yosemite Valley?" "Yes, sir, many and many a time."

"Is it your opinion that a lady can make the journey at the present time?" "One route, so far as I know, is open by which the journey can be made, and that is by Hite's Cove, and if the lady can ride twenty-five or thirty miles in one day over mountains and along precipices and other exciting and dangerous places upon a narrow bridle path, the journey can probably be made."

"Are you willing, in person, to undertake the journey?" "I am."

The woman in question is consulted, and she agrees to make the trial, and a contract is made. Two horses are hitched to a light two seated wagon, into which two of our saddles and light baggage is placed, while one saddle horse is led behind, and we are off from Merced to Mariposa, the termination of our first day's drive. The weather looked fine as we started, and hopefully drove out over the level plain of the San Joaquin Valley amid wide-spreading wheat fields, all crying out for rain.

Towards noon the wind began to rise and the clouds came driving in from the south. Before reaching our dining place, the wind was furious and the whole heavens were surcharged with clouds and dust. We hastened, but 'ere we reached the hospice at Mariposa the rain came down in torrents. We could afford to put up with some discomforts for the great blessing that the rain brought to the land. Mr. Schlageter, a very intelligent German, long resident in California, gave us every attention and made us very comfortable. He was proud of having entertained Senator Trumbull, and said he had had numbers of Milwaukee people as guests in his house, and brought forward his registers for me to look over, and sure enough I ran against our esteemed friends, Mr. and Mrs. William E. Cramer, who were guests with him April 30, 1877. Beside, my worthy host, to show conclusively that he was well-posted about Milwaukee, brought forward a bottle of Milwaukee beer. Our host entertained me long and well with the life and times of Col. Fremont. This was his (Fremont's) home. This was the seat and centre, as it is still, of the celebrated "Mariposa grant," containing some fifty thousand acres of land, and is said to embrace some of the best mineral deposits in the State. The little village bears memorials of Fremont's presence. The main street is called "John street," the next street "Jessie street," and another bears the name of "Benton street," in memory of Col. Benton, the father of Jessie Fremont. It is many years since Col. Fremont sold his claim for $1,500,000. It is now in litigation and scarcely any mining is done in this district, and the town is dead.

The storm had expended itself during the night, and we pushed our journey the next day with muddy roads, and, as we came further on into the mountains, encountering snow fields. But the skies were clear, and, as we slowly came on towards the close of our second day's drive, we reached the brow of the mountain, which overlooked the tremendous gorge, at the bottom of which flowed the Western branch of the Merced River; and in which lay the little mining hamlet sustaining the unpoetic name of "Hite's

Cove." Travelers going into the valley by "Clark's," or the southern route, have many exclamations to make of the wonderfulness of the scene when they first behold the Yosemite from Inspiration Point. But while we did not have that joy, neither have they beheld the wonders of "Hite's Cove." I at once admit the unpoetic character of the name, and demand a change to match that of "Inspiration Point," and suggest that instead of Hite's Cove it be called "Jove's Thunder Factory," or "The Inverted Dome of the Temple of Creation," or some other suited to the glory of the scenery. In passing, let me say that Mr. Hite, who discovered a mine at this point sixteen years ago, has worked it ever since with great success, and is now realizing $600 per day above expenses, and is personally and steadily attending to his business day by day, thus adding to his already large fortune.

Having had to put up with the poor accommodations of a miner's camp, we were not well qualified either by rest or food for the arduous long horseback ride of the third day's journey. Still we were early in the saddle and commenced the ascent by the narrow trail up a steep mountain of two thousand feet. Our horses were true and good. The frost had been sharp over night and the morning air was crisp and cold, imparting great exhilaration as up we went in the presence of the morning sun, which shone directly upon the face of the mountain we were ascending. McLenathan was ahead, while your humble servant brought up the rear.

Some sources of concern and danger attached to this day's ride aside from those common to the route. We were the first party that had been over the road this spring, and so cold and wet has the winter and spring been that little opportunity has been given for the embankments to become dried out and freed from danger of sliding as the weight of the horses came upon them.

And little or no work having been as yet done on the trail, many places had, by the action of detrition, become so narrow that there was but just room for the horses' feet to gain a footing; and when with such a path and with such foundations you must pass along precipices steep down hundreds of feet into yawning abysses, the strain on one's nerves, as well as upon muscle, is calculated to make heavy draft upon mortal strength. We passed long stretches where by no possibility could a horse turn around or the rider alight, and when, if the horse had made a misstep, both horse and rider would have gone to destruction.

We had been misinformed as to a suitable place to stop for our mid-day rest and refreshment. We found only the house of a poor old Irish woman, who had living with her an Italian and a squaw of the Digger tribe of Indians. True, the faint (having unfortunately taken scarcely any breakfast) and weary female of the party could lie down upon the good, generous-hearted old Irish woman's bed, and rest, which she did, and could we then and there have had a good meal of suitable food with a good cup of coffee, it would have helped immensely. All we could get was a piece of sour bread. Suffice it to say that the journey was a long and very hard one, and one which ordinarily had not better be undertaken by a lady. But with the sour bread, two apples, and an occasional rest, we reached, ere the sun was set, the most excellent hotel of Mrs. Leidig, in the Yosemite Valley, the first party of the season with a lady.

This valley was the hiding place of a band of thieving Digger Indians. Somewhere about 1851 or 1852, a military expedition was organized to pursue these mauraders, and in the prosecution of the chase came upon this remarkable valley and were the first to proclaim its existence. More and more since then has it been advertised until it has been visited now by many thousand persons, who I think generally concur in pronouncing it to be among the remarkable specimens of natural curiosity.

The valley is about eight miles long and with an average width of about one mile. It is level and smooth, with many massive trees of oak, pine and cedar growing upon it. In the midst of the valley runs the Merced River, a beautiful stream of considerable size. From this level plain of the valley, which itself is three or four thousand feet above the sea, rise the mountains abruptly and perpendicularly 3,000 feet and more above the level of the valley. The chief of these mountains, "El Capitan," which stands upon the north side of the valley, has a face of a mile, more or less, long, and is as smooth and perfect as if laid up by King Solomon's best workmen. The other mountains, though conjoined and constituting one continuous wall around the circuit of the valley, and rise with nearly equal abruptness and height, are much more irregular, and stand out and in making distinct mountains, suggesting names as the "Sentinel," the "Three Brothers," the "Dome," etc.

As you come close under these vast heights which seem to hang over you, ready to fall upon you, the impression is one of awe and fear beyond expression. The very beautiful, and I may say sublime, features of this scenery are the falls of water which descend from these heights into the vale below and make up the Merced River. Upon the left hand as the valley is entered is the Ribbon Fall, falling 3,300 feet. Upon the right hand comes a fall of less altitude, being only nine hundred feet descent, but having much greater volume of water. This is a very handsome fall and goes by the name of the "Bridal Veil." Next in order upon the left hand comes the Yosemite Fall. This at this season of the year when the snows are melting is a copious stream of water and descends 2,634 feet. Sixteen hundred feet of this fall is made without a break, and the balance is nearly perpendicular.

We ascended the mountain which projects into the valley somewhat like that, over which this cataract pours, a distance of 2,000 feet, where the beholder is directly in front of the pure white, perfect shaft of falling water, a picture unparalleled for beauty, probably, upon the earth's surface. Further up the valley and at its extremity upon the right descends the Merced River proper, creating the Vernal and Nevada Falls. The latter of these is 700 feet high. There is much snow in this part of the valley, and the guides declared we could not reach these Falls. Still we persisted and reached the Vernal which, with its large volume of water now passing from the melted snow, and surrounded as it is with the wildest of scenery, well repaid the effort.

When one remembers that the Falls of Niagara are but 157 feet high, some idea is gained of the extraordinary height of these cataracts. The longer one stands in the presence of this august scenery, the more in grandeur and interest does it grow. Two days was all the time we could devote. We should have been glad to have lingered longer, but other duties beckoned us away.

The Federal Government has conveyed to the State of California the title to this property, as well as that upon which the forest of " Big Trees " stands, and the State has placed the same in charge of a Board of Commissioners who have pnrchased the rights of squatters who had made improvements, paying something over $50,000 for the same, and are making permanent improvements and preserving order in all its parts, thus affording protection and security to travelers. It must ever be a place of resort to all lovers of the grand and beautiful. E. D. H.

LETTER XVI.

*A Review—California Under a . Business Cloud—The Cause—
Ralston—Denis Kearney—The American Settlers—
The Chinese.*

SACRAMENTO, March 28, 1880.

From one end of the State to the other, the cry of "hard times" comes up, from every quarter and from all classes. It is my opinion that with cash in hand the entire real estate of California can be purchased to-day for just one-half that it could have been five years ago, or before the failure of the Bank of California. That event, to-wit: the failure of that bank, was the first great blow to the abnormal condition of things which then existed, and had for a long time before, in this State. Wm. C. Ralston, the head and front of that institution, was a self-made man of great native courage, energy, vast endurance, great application with dispatch of business, generous to a fault, and yet unscrupulous, headstrong and wholly unsound in morals. For years he moved in the zenith of business influence and power. He claimed for California that she was exceptionally favored in all natural endowments of wealth. The precious metals, according to his theory, were abundant and inexhaustible; the climatic forces, for the blessings of the race, without a parallel—the land yielding with the smallest touch of industry in the greatest abundance the most precious fruits, the great sea opening fresh virgin markets to the ends of the earth. Therefore magnify, build high, build broad, build deep and long. His ear and his hand were open to consider and help forward any reasonably well considered scheme that had for its object the aggrandizement of California. Had he combined with his many good qualities that of high moral integrity, which must always be set as a watch dog over man's lower nature, he might have proved a great blessing instead of a curse to California. Too many of the bright, smart men of California have been personally immoral, especially in the direction of licentiousness. An accomplished and experienced woman of the world told me that Ralston had eighteen wives beside his lawful wife. Ralston having used the funds of the bank wrongfully, if not criminally, to carry forward his grand schemes, until its five millions of stock were consumed, was removed from his high place, and the same day went down to the beach, where the great ocean and the Bay of San Francisco mingle their waters at the Golden Gate, and drowned himself, a man in the prime of life, with a splendid physique, and with more friends and admirers to-day than almost any man that has ever lived in the State.

From that period to this the State of California has been waning from that point to which her fancied consequence had carried her. Imperceptibly at first, but steadily has she declined. Her mineral interests had been magnified by stock speculation five or ten times more than the real facts and condition of things justified. Through this channel came vast millions from London, some from Paris, Berlin and Hamburg, and much from New York. These moneys have entered into the great mining schemes, not only, but into other vast California enterprises, and but a small percentage, probably, ever got back. The process of sending money here for investment as in those gala days of the Ralston era has gradually subsided until now it is ended, and all schemes are left to get on as best they can, and Californians now are not ashamed to wear old clothes and talk about the sober virtues of economy and frugality; and hence, if I judge aright, the era of their true prosperity is now to begin, and will go forward on a far better basis than ever before. But she has some difficulties to encounter and surmount ere general prosperity will be established. The former free-and-easy way of living with floods of money to be had on easy terms except the rates of interest, which were always enormous, led the whole community to regard being in debt as no serious affair. Hence nearly everybody is in debt. Some of the very best men in the State, possessed of large properties, are heavily involved. Many of these men cannot pay, and great estates are upon the market on every hand. This is true of country and landed estates, as well as city property. This makes room for a new class of men, with moderate means, and truer ideas of business pursuits to come in, and will greatly tend to magnify the country population and to promote the agricultural interest, which is by far the higher and better interest of the State. This old condition of things has resulted in drawing too many persons into the city and towns. Particularly is San Francisco too large for the legitimate needs of the State,—a city of one half the size could do all the business that properly comes to her door. I doubt if she has any more real legitimate business than Milwaukee. Certainly if the signs hung out, "To Let," are any token of an overdone condition, it is patent in San Francisco. Every other building in the city seems to be so labeled. Hence the Denis Kearneys and his crowd of idle men.

By the way, I went to see Denis and had two lengthy conversations with him. If you would be interested to know about the personnel of this somewhat noted agitator, let me say that he is a man of thirty-five years of age, well preserved, of small stature, and very modest and moderate presence, and of strictly temperate habits. He dresses plainly in dark blue, is rather dark complexioned, speaks low and soft in private conversation. I accompanied him to the Sand Lots, and heard him deliver one of his addresses to the crowd of twenty-five hundred, who stood quietly and decently before him. His address was written, word for word, as, he told me, his speeches always were written. His voice on the platform is strong, clear and effective. He speaks with deliberation and at times with no small force.

I asked Mr. Kearney what was to be the outcome of all this agitation. He replied that it all "looked dark to him," and in a general way prophesied some fearful revolution in affairs.

While the agitation of which he has been a prominent leader here in California has wrought out in the new constitution some new and, as I am inclined to think, useful reforms, there its usefulness ended, and Denis Kearney should have gone back to his dray and asked his friends to join him, and, if there was not employment in overdone San Francisco, led them forth on to vacant land, of which there are millions of acres lying idle, and gone to planting and reaping, and thus had bread and to spare. Then might he have become a benefactor as well as an agitator and a blessing to workingmen.

I endeavored to point out to him some of these paths, through, or into which, he might lead his adherents from the wilderness of poverty and find plentiful reward to honest industry. But he did not seem to take any interest in such a proposition—but chooses, I fear, rather to stand forth as a somewhat aimless agitator. I venture to prophesy that from this time on his star will wane. That his tirade against the Chinese, against capitalists and corporations has been somewhat disastrous I make no doubt. That it has sent some capital away and deterred some from coming to California is doubtless true. But that is not California's chief trouble or cause of her present depressed condition. Overtrading and an altogether exaggerated estimate of her mineral consequence, which has led the great proportion of her population to become speculators, and to turn aside from, or rather never to have adopted the sober walks of industry, is rather to be credited with the evil.

The desire to become suddenly rich has overborne all the bounds of sound discretion and wrecked thousands of very capable men, and they stand along the highway of life, many of them in grim despair, and refuse to take up the burden of manual labor.

It was an extraordinary vote which the people of California gave in their late election upon the Chinese question. Less than a thousand votes were cast in their favor. And yet when many of those who voted for their exclusion are pointed to the industrious and frugal habits of these people—to their temperate, dignified and respectable behavior as a whole, to the productive nature of their labor—they begin to apologize for their act. That there are some evils growing out of the presence of so large a number of alien population of only one sex is evident on the face of things, and that a proper national regulation of the question is probably advisable, if not necessary.

But to-day California cannot dispense with her Chinese population without being thrown back for years in her industrial interests. No Denis Kearneys will, or can, supply the deficiency.

California possesses in her climate and soil unparalleled sources of human comfort and welfare. All that her people need to do to secure that end is to quit stock gambling and all other speculative pursuits, and go to honest labor in the mines and, more especially, to the land. Here is her chief wealth. Let her Legislature inaugurate a system of irrigation, which is perfectly practicable, and such is the capacity of her soil and the preciousness of its products that the time would be brief ere the song of comfort, peace and plenty would be heard in all her borders.

My impression is, from all I hear after my three months sojourn, and mingling with many of her frank and generous hearted people, that public sentiment is crystalizing into a conviction that sober industry must take the place of speculation; that labor must supplant idleness, knowledge ignorance, and that virtue must take the place of vice. These conditions accepted, and the prosperty of any community is assured. E. D. H.

www.ingramcontent.com/pod-product-compliance
Lightning Source LLC
Chambersburg PA
CBHW020256090426
42735CB00009B/1099